REPEAL AND REPLACE AMERICA
THE LEFT'S STRATEGY TO
FUNDAMENTALLY TRANSFORM AMERICA

Jim Spurlock

Repeal and Replace America

The Left's Strategy to Fundamentally Transform America

©2020 Jim Spurlock

print ISBN: 978-1-09832-070-6

ebook ISBN: 978-1-09832-071-3

CONTENTS

What follows is for those who want to "Make America Great Again," to prevent it from becoming what the left, democrats all, believes it should be … a liberal, progressive, irreligious, pro-abortion, amoral, unconstitutional, borderless, God-free, gun-free, socialist deep-state, i.e., a "partocracy", run by them.

FYI a partocracy is a government run by a political party or factions; totalitarianism; socialism; communism, like in Russia, Cuba, Venezuela, and China… rather than by individuals or representatives of the people, like the Constitutional Republic of the United States of America.

The far left, all Democrats, sees these things, not necessarily as desirable end states, rather as catalysts toward repealing (destroying) America and replacing it with a rational utopian socialist society with peace and justice for all, and

> "…reflecting a radical new Democratic Party that views our nation as a rogue state, in which everything must be destroyed and remade: our laws, our institutions, our freedoms, our history and our values" – Tucker Carlson.

This is consistent with Karl Marx's original aspiration for all mankind … i.e., after a period of destruction of the current order, followed by chaos and totalitarianism, people would eventually relent, give up their property, their wives and families, their careers, their wealth, and agree to live an egalitarian peaceful co-existence with fellow travelers, where each person has a government job, works according to his ability, and is paid according to his need. Marx considered this "social evolution" to be inevitable and the only just end to an unjust World. Likewise, modern Democrat Socialists like Sanders, Obama, Biden, Pelosi, AOC, and Warren see the same fate for an unjust America.

Most Americans, especially Millennials are ignorant of what follows, and Ronald Reagan said "Our liberal friends know so much that isn't so", but as they say, "knowledge is the beginning of wisdom", so let us begin.

Karl Marx, a sincere young social justice warrior and intellectual, sought to remedy the grave economic injustices he saw in his day. Thing is, since Marx wrote the Communist Manifesto in 1848, there has not be one single success story, but over 100 million people have been impoverished, starved, frozen, raped, tortured, imprisoned, or killed pursuing his utopian dream state.

Despite the lessons of history, "Marxism has come to the United States as Liberalism", so said Ronald Reagan. What we see in our institutions and society today is the result of 100 years of progressive activism, not just a recent pendulum swing in right/left politics. As you will see the left's ideology, goals, strategies, and tactics go all the way back to the early 20th century and originated inside the Soviet Communist Party which desired world domination, with only the United States of America standing in its way. The 45 Communist Goals for the destruction of America from the inside revealed in the book, *The Naked Communist*, will be discussed and put in historical perspective, and made relevant to the 2020 election.

For conservative republicans who can't understand how or why liberal democrats think and act the way they do, this book will be revealing … shining light on the darkness of the left's hundred-year communist heritage and modern-day game plan to fundamentally transform America … an unpleasant truth. It is perhaps not so ironic that the Greek word for left is sinister!

For liberal democrats who can't understand how or why conservative republicans think and act the way they do, this book may be revolting … expressing conservative's rational disdain for their illicit, amoral, illegal, clandestine, subversive, communist goals and agenda to liberalize all societal institutions, take down the duly elected president, and establish a utopian socialist Amerika, run by them. Most do not realize it but there really is a vast left-wing conspiracy.

For apolitical independent families and friends who can't understand why we all can't just get along, this book will be educational ... explaining the great political divide and why they should vote wisely in 2020. Conservative republicans and open-minded Independents are asked to recommend this book to as many such people as possible and encourage them to read it with an open mind, then encourage meaningful discussion.

Elon Musk, of Tesla and SpaceX fame, said on May 18, "Take the red pill!"

> "The red pill and blue pill is a meme representing a choice between taking either a 'red pill' that reveals an unpleasant truth, or taking a 'blue pill' to remain in blissful ignorance. The terms are directly derived from a scene in the 1999 film The Matrix." —Wikipedia

That is what you'll be doing if you read this book ... you'll be taking the red pill...suffering an unpleasant truth!

Liberal democrats who refuse to read it have likely already taken the blue pill ... content in blissful ignorance.

THE VAST LEFT-WING CONSPIRACY EMERGES FROM THE SHADOWS

In 2016, the deep state was positioned, sleeper cells were activated, useful idiots were engaged, the fake news was busy, and the election was rigged ... but then along came the man they didn't count on, Donald J. Trump, and just like that—America was back.

Who is the left anyway? Who is the deep state? What are sleeper cells? Who are useful idiots? What do they want? Why is the left suddenly so hostile toward the right? Why do they hate the president so viscerally? What is at stake if they succeed?

FYI ... The phrase "useful idiots" sounds like something Trump would come up with to ridicule his enemies, but it was Lenin and Stalin's name for communist admirers in the American press, movies, academia, and government who were useful to the communist cause. They called them idiots because these fashionable liberals in the 30s, 40s, and 50s didn't have a clue what they were really supporting—hard core, murderous, revolutionary communists disguised as social justice warriors. It is still a good description today for bleeding heart liberals who support democratic socialism, most also without a clue. Useful idiots have all taken the blue pill!

This is the true story of how, over the past hundred years, Soviet communists and American liberals colluded to embed their socialist ideology, disguised as progressivism, into every institution of American life without most Americans even realizing it.

A key strategy of Marxism is to destroy what exists to make room for the socialist utopia to follow. To them the pain is worth the gain; the end justifies the means. There is no crime they are not willing to commit, and no lie they are not willing to tell in pursuing their leftist agenda. The last four years, 2016–2020, of shenanigans by congressional democrats, the Obama/Biden DOJ and FBI, and their comrades in the liberal media are proof of that point. Obama's goal seemed to be to cripple America so it could never be great again, i.e., double the national debt, Obamacare, Paris Climate Accord, Iran Nuke Deal, TPP, ISIS, etc. ... while VP Biden blackmailed Ukraine and courted communist China to enrich his family and friends. But all this is just the tip of the iceberg.

The communist goals for the destruction of America from within, adopted many decades ago, are presented here in context of the left's recognizable progressive achievements such as the liberalization of our universities, courts, press, movies, radio, TV, churches, art, morality, culture, unions, big tech, congress, marriage, and many others. These transformational achievements are self-evident truths to any mature informed adult, this book's audience. Most millennials are oblivious to this fact because it is all they have ever known, and their minds have been plied for decades by liberal influencers in schools, media, music, church, TV/radio/movies. The latest Fox poll shows that 69 percent of millennials prefer liberal socialism to conservative capitalism, i.e., free stuff and sharing to freedom and achievement.

Amerika was a miniseries broadcast in 1987 about life in the United States after a bloodless takeover engineered by the Soviet Union. The miniseries focused on the demoralized U.S. people a decade after the Soviet conquest. The miniseries was fiction but the communist goals for the transformation of America and their pursuit by the far-left Democratic Socialist Party of 2020 are not!

You will be shocked, you will be informed, you will be glad, and you may be sad you read *Repeal and Replace America – The Left's Strategy to Fundamentally Transform America* … as President-elect Obama promised he would do. Biden is now saying the same thing on TV. Bernie says he wants to not just beat Trump but "transform the country." Representative James Clyburn (D-SC), who saved Biden's primary run, says the democrats should "use the pandemic crisis to reshape the country to their vision."

So, just what do they want to transform America into, and what is their vision for America? Trump says, "Make America Great Again," but what does that really mean? When was it great and why? The country is greatly divided, but are the two sides really that incompatible? Can't we all just get along?

To answer those questions, we must look back into history and bring it forward. To see where the left wants to take us, we need to understand where they are coming from. To see what Trump means by "Again," we need to understand when and why America was ever great in the first place.

TESTIMONY ABOUT THE BOOK

This is the professional editing evaluation from publisher of *The Naked Communist*, Izzard Ink: "The author shows notable writing skills, able to communicate with clarity and get a point across with clean, well-structured sentences. Paragraphs flow nicely, and its usually clear what point is being made. There is potential because the writing itself is of high quality."

Dennis Prager, conservative radio talk show host, author, video (PragerU) and movie (No Safe Spaces) producer says,

> "Jim, feel free to quote me as much as you like. Your book sounds excellent and important. I wish you much success. America needs more people like you." Best wishes, Dennis.

Frank Hawkins, who was a captain in Army Intelligence, served as a case officer in clandestine collection operations for the Defense Intelligence Agency during the Cold War in Germany, and he says, "Jim, this is right on target. As you are making clear, The Naked Communist is a total manifesto for what is going on."

Dr. Ben Carson says, of the 2017 edition of *The Naked Communist*, the cornerstone of this book "*The Naked Communist* lays out the whole progressive agenda."

Ronald Reagan, who knew its author, says, "You'll be shocked, you will be informed, and you'll be glad you heard W. Cleon Skousen."

You will hear a lot from W. Cleon Skousen in this book.

FOREWORD

The author started his career in August 1969 with a major steel company. While commie-type-hippies and bohemian proletariats like Bernie were partying, smoking weed, and loving each other up at the first Woodstock music festival, I graduated from Auburn University in Applied Physics and was driving from Auburn, AL, to Ashland, KY, with a wife and young child to start my first job at a large steel mill.

The steel company put out a monthly newsletter to all employees about company business, financial matters, technology, and other things related to steel production. The newsletter also included descriptions of political issues that effected the company's wellbeing, including how politicians voted on such issues. I noticed a trend that democrats voted against the interest of the company and for the interest of the unions almost a hundred percent of the time. Republicans did just the opposite. This was across about a dozen states.

I tracked these statistics for several years and wondered why this was the case. Coming from the deep south, Alabama, we had a natural bias against "liberals," but most southerners were democrats back then, so I was confused. How could this be, such statistically significant bias against one of America's critical industries by democrats, and a bias toward the United Steelworkers Union which I had come to disdain. I began to ask others if they notice the same thing and had any explanation for it.

Various explanations were offered but then a friend and associate gave me a book and said, read this and you will understand. It was around 1975, the Vietnam War was over, LBJ was gone, Nixon had resigned in disgrace, the Environmental Protection Agency (EPA) was established, and the counterculture movement and Great Society programs were in full sway. I was not political back then and didn't really care about politics, but I did care about my career and it appeared democrats were voting against my own best-interests most of the time.

The book my friend gave me to read was *The Naked Communist* by a former FBI agent W. Cleon Skousen. Skousen, an associate and confidant of J. Edgar Hoover, who had written this definitive work on communism, first published in 1958 and used by the FBI, CIA, and military intelligence to help the agents understand the existential threat this new post World War II scourge represented. My copy was the 1961 edition which contained not only the history of Marxist Communism and their goals for world domination but a specific list of forty-five Soviet goals for the destruction of America from the inside.

Out of all the goals, one was "Capture one of both political parties in the United States," and another was "Infiltrate and gain control of more unions." There it was it all made sense now. Could it be that the democratic party had been "captured" and the United Steelworkers Union had been "infiltrated"? Those two goals alone would not have made the case, but all combined produced a pattern of evidence that was compelling.

The other goals seemed consistent with what I observed about liberal politics and societal changes in those days. It was disturbing that so many things I saw going on regarding schools, unions, morality, churches, religion, family, constitution, history, courts, academia, riots, press, radio/TV/pictures, culture, art, business, police, violence, and race were seemingly planned and executed by Soviet communists and American sympathizers decades earlier! This was a disturbing thought, and still is!

Because ... it was not a prophecy; it was planning, which means it was premeditated and executed deliberately and with enthusiasm ... and way too statistically significant to be happenstance. Prophecy is an inspired revelation of a future truth, like in the Old Testament. Prediction is foretelling the future based on analysis of the past and present, like weather forecasting. Planning is setting goals to influence the future, i.e., bias the outcome. Planning is what the forty-five goals of communism are about. They are instructions, to future generations, a roadmap, a game plan with a specific outcome in mind ... the transformation of traditional America into a liberal Marxist socialist state, like the Soviet Union. That these goals have been so successfully achieved today is evidence of decades of premeditated activism by the left, now all democrats.

Shortly after digesting *The Naked Communist*, and almost choking on its disturbing revelations, my same friend gave me a copy of Saul Alinsky's *Rules for Radicals: A Pragmatic Primer for Realistic Radicals*. The book begins with, "What follows is for those who want to change the world from what it is to what they believe it should be." Alinsky developed the "community organizer" model for infiltrating and transforming institutions without violent confrontation. It is the model Barack Obama and Hillary Clinton used to make it to the top and is still the gold standard for party operatives today.

I was a naïve young man in many ways in 1975, but a wise elderly friend at church told me I was an old soul. I did not know what he meant, but I do now. I often see things that others do not and seem to have a natural ability to cut through the drivel and blather and get to the bottom of things, to connect the dots, to see the big picture. This God-given ability, enhanced by my STEM education in physics, and professional experiences have served me and others well, although it is not usually appreciated by liberals and emotional individuals who defer to feelings, decorum, and intention over facts, logic, and achievement ... like those who swoon over Obama but cringe at Trump.

I may have been naïve in many ways, but I was analytical enough to begin to connect the dots of a pattern of evidence to lead me to some startling and disturbing conclusions over the next several decades.

Connecting the dots was what our intelligence agencies failed to do prior to the Islamic terrorist attacks on 9/11/01. If we fail again to connect the dots, and democrats prevail in 2020, I believe the impact on America will be far more catastrophic and long-lasting than 9/11.

2020 is unarguably the most politically divided, viscerally contentious, and consequentially decisive time in America since the Civil War. We will document how the democratic party, once the party of slavery, Jim Crow, and KKK, became the party of socialism, Barak Obama, and Antifa.

If ever there could be a time to advance a theory of a vast left-wing conspiracy against traditional conservative America, this is it—the forty-five communist goals are the smoking gun, and 2020 democrats are holding it! Their relentless pursuit of these anti-American progressive goals by overt and covert means since the 60s violates their oath of office and the constitution, and it is time to expose them and hold them accountable. Their illegal, illegitimate, felonious, immoral, clandestine activities to defeat candidate Donald Trump, protect Hillary Clinton, frame and prosecute General Michael Flynn, and then take down duly elected President Trump are proof positive of their intentions to act outside the constitution and the law to achieve their goals.

Update as at March 15, 2020: About two dozen Obama administration officials, including quid pro Joe Biden, have been outed as having unmasked General Flynn's legitimate classified communications with the Russian ambassador during the transition, and then leaked them to the fake news media. This is a felony carrying a ten-year term in prison for the leaker, but they are all complicit. The FBI with instructions from the highest levels then set a perjury trap for General Flynn to get him fired or jailed, the ultimate purpose of which was to get to President Trump. Their clandestine scheme, the "insurance policy," is all coming out now and hopefully will be prosecuted by Attorney General Barr and U.S. Attorney John Durham soon.

Let the reader understand that these recent high-profile events are not just illegal activities by a few rogue agents, like Watergate was. These activities represent the culmination of a long history of fundamental transformation of the Democratic Party of JFK into the Democratic Socialist Party of Obama, Clinton, Sanders, Biden, AOC, Pelosi, and Schumer. We will examine the background and long history of democrats' seduction by communism/socialism, and how the seduced have now become the seducers.

So, forty-five years after seeing the first evidence I'm prepared to prosecute the case that the Democratic party has been "captured" by communism, adopted socialism, and embraced rascalism … and that they should be indicted and tried for their crimes against America. I shall indict them with the contents of this book but you the voter will have to convict them at the ballot box in November by voting the bastards out of office.

Perhaps AG Barr and U.S. Attorney Durham will indict and prosecute some them in court, but I'm not holding my breath. Democrats are mostly lawyers and have proven to be Teflon offenders … nothing sticks to them. Like unrepentant domestic terrorist Bill Ayers, Obama's buddy, said of himself, "guilty as sin, free as a bird."

ABSTRACT

America has been under attack for the last hundred years by socialist ideologs who want to fundamentally transform America from what it is, a religious, conservative, free enterprise, capitalist republic, to what they believe it should be, an irreligious, liberal, centrally managed, socialist partocracy. And they have made remarkable progress!

The modern Democratic Socialist Party is the latest incarnation of this evolution toward repealing and replacing America the beautiful, the land of the free and the home of the brave, with Amerika the bountiful, the land of free stuff and the home of the slave. This is the fundamental goal of leftist progressives everywhere.

Socialist ideology, which has its roots in Karl Marx's *Communist Manifesto*, first found its footing in the Russian Revolution of 1917 and was admired by many American elites, intellectuals, academics, entertainment, and media types who saw it as a grand social justice movement. During and after the Great Depression, 1929–1942, some Americans in high places decided Soviet socialism would be an alternative worth exploring and defected to serve Moscow by infiltrating the Roosevelt and Truman administrations, universities, Hollywood, and the News Media. After World War II, Soviet communists and their willing comrades in America adopted forty-five goals for the transformation of America from the inside. These were compatible with the thinking of liberal elites of the day ... and still are! Following Marx and Lenin's strategy to "first burn down what is, then build upon the ashes" … to make way for the socialist utopia to come, the Goals included things like:

#15. "Capture one or both political parties in the United States."

#16. "Use technical decisions of the courts to weaken basic American institutions…"

#17. "Get control of the schools. Use them as transmission belts for socialism and communist propaganda. Soften the curriculum. Get control of teacher's associations. Put the party line in textbooks."

#18. "Gain control of all student newspapers."

#19. "Use student riots to foment public protests…"

#20. "Infiltrate the press. Get control of book-review assignments, editorial writing, and policy-making positions."

#21. "Gain control of key positions in radio, TV, and motion pictures."

#22. "Continue discrediting American culture by degrading all forms of artistic expression…replacing good sculpture with shapeless, awkward, meaningless forms."

#23. "…promote ugliness, repulsive, meaningless art."

#24. "Eliminate all laws governing obscenity by calling them censorship and violation of free speech and free press."

#25. "Break down cultural standards of morality by promoting pornography and obscenity in books, magazines, motions pictures, radio and TV."

#26. "Present homosexuality, degeneracy and promiscuity as 'normal, natural, and healthy."

#27. "Infiltrate the churches and replace revealed religion with "social" religion. Discredit the Bible and emphasize the need for intellectual maturity which does not need a "religious crutch."

#28. "Eliminate prayer or any phase of religious expression in schools on the grounds it violates "separation of church and state."

#29. "Discredit the American Constitution by calling it inadequate, old-fashioned, out of step with modern needs…"

#30. "Discredit the American founding fathers. Present them as selfish aristocrats who had no concern for the 'common man."

#31. "Belittle all forms of American culture and discourage the teaching of American history…"

#32. "Support any socialist movement to give centralized control over any part of the culture – education, social agencies, welfare programs, mental health, etc."

#35. "Discredit and eventually dismantle the FBI."

#36. "Infiltrate and gain control of more unions."

#37. "Infiltrate and gain control of big business."

#38. "Transfer some of the powers of arrest from police to social agencies…"

#40. "Discredit the family as an institution. Encourage promiscuity and easy divorce."

#41. "Emphasize the need to raise children away from the negative influence of parents…"

#42. "Create the impression that violence and insurrection are legitimate aspects of the American tradition; that students and special interest groups should rise up and use 'united force' to solve economic, political or social problems." – George Floyd protests/riots anyone?… or Watts, Berkeley, Rodney King, Ferguson, '68 Democratic Convention

Many of these will sound familiar in light of recent events.

Older readers who have watched the changes to America, the gradual but relentless shift to the left, over the past five decades, should be saying…"Oh, My, God…you mean to tell me all those fundamental transformations to American society and institutions I've witnessed and lamented over my life were actually planned by old school Soviet Communists and American Liberals who sought to destroy America and replace it with Amerika, a communist socialist partocracy like the Soviet Union. We've been had!" Yes, that's exactly what this book is about. These Goals and agenda have been fully embraced by the modern Democratic Socialist Party of Barack Obama, Joe Biden, Hillary Clinton, Bernie Sanders, Nancy Pelosi, Chuck Schumer. AOC, Omar, the Congressional Black Caucus, the mainstream fake-news media, Hollywood, Academia, Universities, big tech business (Facebook, Amazon, Google, Twitter, etc.). One can argue whether the Goals are worthy of pursuing or not but cannot argue their origin. They unquestionably came from a distant generation of Soviet communists intent on repealing and replacing America! That should give any voter, republican or democrat, pause in 2020.

These are unquestionably modern "liberal and progressive" ideas but are originally from a book first published in 1958 by former FBI agent W. Cleon Skousen, a best seller in its day, *The Naked Communist*, now updated in 2017. (Reprinted in this book with permission from the W. Cleon Skousen Library and Izzard Ink Publishing Company.)

When they use terms like "Get control…" or "Infiltrate…" or "Support…" or "Eliminate…" or "Discredit…," or "Dismantle…," it is always with malevolent intent! Burn it down! Overwhelm it!

Keep in mind these may just sound like recent "liberal" ideas, but in fact they were conceived many decades ago by Soviet communists hell bent on destroying America from the inside. There can be no dispute that liberal, i.e., communist/socialist ideology has permeated our schools, universities, academia, curricula, news media, entertainment, courts, churches, politics, and most institutions that form the fabric of American society in the twenty-first century. These "liberals" have removed prayer from schools, the Ten Commandments from the courtroom, every mention of faith and God from the new six-hundred-million-dollar Capital welcome center, redefined traditional marriage and family, promoted late-term abortion, dominated our universities, brainwashed our youth, created the fake news, socialized our health care, produced a welfare state, discredited our FBI, and much much more.

All 45 Goals were read into the congressional record in 1963 at the height of the cold war. Only one has yet to be achieved. Those which have been, like those mentioned earlier, are still having profoundly negative impacts on America. Saul Alinsky, an American commie activist and "community organizer," from the 50s and 60s, rewrote the democrats' playbook in 1971, *Rules for Radicals*, and passed his subversive ideas on to the next generation of activists like Hillary Clinton and Barack Obama.

True communists are about violent revolution, not peaceful evolution. Socialists who live in a democracy like America must be more subtle and patient. Alinsky advised them on how to organize by infiltration, not by open conflict. But the crowd of democrat candidates for president and Congress today have lost discipline, and despite warnings from Pelosi and even Obama to cool it, to not give away their real agenda until they are in power, they are galvanizing their opponents by unjustly attacking our president, failing to achieve anything for the country, and openly campaigning as socialists with an agenda that would make Alinsky cringe. Now they are leveraging the coronavirus pandemic to get funding for their favorite liberal causes, having nothing to do with the virus relief efforts and using their power in democratic-controlled states to crater the Trump economy like they have not been able to do by other means. We'll see what happens, but I believe it will backfire on them because Trump is playing chess while they are playing checkers.

Below the surface and below most people's radar the left has, over many decades, weaponized the weather, education, immigration, energy, race, drugs, guns, news, entertainment, sports, religion, courts, trade, foreign policy, military, culture, morality, marriage, congress, welfare, health care, unions, school boards, big business, the FBI/CIA, family and children, and more to serve their progressive socialist agenda, i.e., progress toward repealing and replacing America—repealing what it is and replacing it with they believe it should be … a godless, irreligious, borderless, liberal, amoral, socialist partocracy which controls every aspect of our lives, just like in every communist/socialist country that has ever existed … where America is not First among Winners, but Amerika is Last among Losers!

This sounds bad, so why would the left want to do this to America, they live here too. They live here but they hate the idea of America, America's founders, America's institutions, American exceptionalism, the American Dream, and America First. Sound like any couple you know, like the Obamas maybe.

Perhaps the most egregious recent example is a new bill proposed in December 2019 by over forty-four democrat House members, including all four of AOC's squad. It's called the New Way Forward Act (H.R. 5383). According to Fox News commentator Tucker Carlson, "It would be the *coup de grâce* to our already balkanized country, reflecting a radical new Democratic Party that views our nation as a rogue state, in which everything must be destroyed and remade: our laws, our institutions, our freedoms, our history and our values." This book will provide deep insight into why that statement is deemed, "Mostly True," even according to liberal shill, Snopes. This bill will not pass any time soon but represents the aspirations of the new-left National Democratic Party which will continue to push its agenda through democratic party channels until they overwhelm the system or burn it down.

America is a rogue state, destroy and remake, burn it down, build upon the ashes, repeal and replace—as you will see this is the communist way and has been since Karl Marx and Friedrich Engels wrote the *Communist Manifesto* in 1848 … and now it's the Democratic Socialist way.

This book will prosecute the case that the left, all democrats in 2020, owe their ideology, methods, strategies, and goals to their patriarchs, Karl Marx, V.I. Lenin, and Joseph Stalin, that their aim is to fundamentally transform America, and that their aggressive pursuit of the forty-five goals of communism for the destruction of America over the past sixty years is the smoking gun that proves the case.

CHAPTER I
THE GREAT POLITICAL DIVIDE—2016-2020

Before Donald J. Trump had even been inaugurated, many Hillary Clinton voters were so apoplectic, angry, disappointed, and in shock that they had ceased communicating with friends, and even family members, who voted for Donald Trump. The author experienced this first-hand. Several people who voted for Trump called the Dennis Prager show to tell him that their daughters had informed them they would no longer allow their parents to see their grandchildren. A wife from Denver informed their mother that her husband should not communicate with their teenage children unless they were present. And one man sent him an e-mail reporting that his brother-in-law's mother told him that she "no longer had a son."

The current impeachment of our president has inflamed passions on both sides, but anti-Trump liberals seem to be more aggressive and willing to offend than pro-Trump conservatives. As Newt Gingrich said, "It's gone too far now and can only end when one side wins and the other loses." The left is dug in and determined to defend the "progress" it has made over the past sixty years. This country has not been this divided and seen such hatred and vitriol since perhaps the Civil War.

The author is not one of those polite conservatives willing to bend over and take it from obnoxious aggressive anti-Trump liberals. My policy is to never let a liberal get the last word! But that policy requires some flexibility since you can pick your friends, but you cannot pick your relatives. I cut that accommodation off at the immediate family.

How did we get here? Why is the reaction to an election so visceral this time, like no other since the election of Lincoln during the Civil War days? Did Trump's bombastic ways create this division, or did the underlying division create Trump? Dinesh D'souza argues for the latter, and so do I.

In this book, I will argue that the foundational ideology of modern leftism comes from Karl Marx, mid-nineteenth century, and Soviet communism, early twentieth century, and has now been fully embraced in the new Democratic Socialist Party. Millennials will disagree because they do not know what they don't know. As presented to them in schools and universities today, Marx and Engels are to be admired, and Washington and Jefferson were white, male, sexist, racist, slave owners. For example, Barry Soetoro, aka Barack Hussein Obama, was raised by communists and Muslims, hates traditional conservative America like they did, and admitted in his book he sought out Marxist professors and radical students in college. At Occidental, Columbia, and Harvard he did not have to look far!

Both Obama and Hillary Clinton are fans and students of Saul Alinsky, who wrote the new left's playbook *Rules for Radicals*, which advocates infiltration of all social institutions, acquisition of power by deception and subterfuge, then change from the top. Obama, an obscure articulate black man with no real accomplishments in his life, used Alinsky methods to make it to the top. Hillary was to follow … but then along came Donald Trump and his band of deplorables. Decades of "progress" were shut down over night … and to quote Forest Gump, "just like that" conservative America was back. The left, democrats, socialists, communists, brainwashed students, liberal elites, academia, news media, entertainment, Big Tech, and their fellow travelers and comrades hate Trump, and his deplorables, for it.

CHAPTER 2
DENNIS PRAGER'S WIT AND WISDOM

Dennis Prager, of Prager U, and one of the most astute political thinkers of our day, has some other thoughts on reasons for the great political divide also. I've included this information here with Dennis's permission and blessing.

Ten Reasons Left-Wingers Cut Trump Voters from Their Lives
By Dennis Prager (November 29, 2016). See www. prageru.com to see an amazing library of brief but profound videos, and please contribute to keep them free and available to all.

Here are ten reasons left-wingers cut Trump voters from their lives. (Emphasis added.)

1. "Just like our universities shut out conservative ideas and speakers, more and more individuals on the left now shut out conservative friends and relatives as well as conservative ideas.

2. Many, if not most, leftists have been indoctrinated with leftism their entire lives. This is easily shown. There are far more conservatives who read articles, who listen to and watch

left-wing broadcasts, and who have studied under left-wing teachers than there are people on the left who have read, listened to, or watched anything of the right or who have taken classes with conservative instructors. As a result, those on the left really believe that those on the right are all sexist, intolerant, xenophobic, homophobic, Islamophobic, racist, and bigoted. Not to mention misogynistic and transphobic. *(Hillary calls these a basket of deplorables.)*

3. Most left-wing positions are emotion-based. That's a major reason people who hold leftist views will sever relations with people they previously cared for or even loved. Their emotions (in this case, irrational fear and hatred) simply overwhelm them. *(It's hard to debate politics with a lefty because after they run out of logical/factual things to say, they usually go emotional on you…Shift the subject, Ignore the facts, Call you names, Kill the messenger, Obsess, and Overreact. The acronym is SICKO, watch for it)*

4. Since Karl Marx, leftists have loved ideas more than people. All Trump voters who have been cut off by children, in-laws, and lifelong friends now know how true that is.

5. People on the right think that most people on the left are wrong; people on the left think that most people on the right are evil. *(I felt this way before the impeachment coup, but now I'm leaning toward "Evil" for democrats.)* Decades of labeling conservative positions as "hateful" and labeling conservative individuals as "sexist," "intolerant," "xenophobic," "homophobic," "racist," and "bigoted" have had their desired effect.

6. The left associates human decency not so much with personal integrity as with having correct—i.e., progressive—political positions. Therefore, if you don't hold progressive

positions, you lack decency. Ask your left-wing friends if they'd rather their high-school son or daughter cheat on tests or support Trump.

7. Most individuals on the left are irreligious, so the commandment "Honor your father and your mother" means nothing to those who have cut off relations with parents because they voted for Trump.

8. Unlike conservatives, politics gives most leftists' lives meaning. Climate change is a good example. For leftists, fighting carbon emissions means saving human existence on earth. Now, how often does anyone get a chance to literally save the world? Therefore, to most leftists, if you voted for Trump, you have both negated their reason for living and are literally destroying the planet. Why would they have Thanksgiving or Christmas with such a person?

9. The left tends toward the totalitarian. And every totalitarian ideology seeks to weaken the bonds between children and parents. The left seeks to dilute parental authority and replace it with school authority and government authority. So, when your children sever their bond with you because you voted for Trump, they are acting like the good totalitarians the left has molded.

10. While there are kind and mean individuals on both sides of the political spectrum, as a result of all the above, there are more mean people on the left than on the right. What other word than "mean" would anyone use to describe a daughter who banished her parents from their grandchildren's lives because of their vote?"

Then there is Trump derangement syndrome.

"Trump derangement syndrome (TDS) is a term for criticism of negative reactions to United States President Donald Trump that are perceived to be irrational and have little regard towards Trump's actual policy positions, or actions undertaken by his administration. The term has been used by Trump supporters to discredit criticism of his actions, as a way of reframing the discussion by suggesting that his opponents are incapable of accurately perceiving the world." —Wikipedia

"The origin of the term is traced to political columnist and commentator Charles Krauthammer, a psychiatrist, who originally coined the phrase Bush derangement syndrome in 2003 during the presidency of George W. Bush. That 'syndrome' was defined by Krauthammer as 'the acute onset of paranoia in otherwise normal people in reaction to the policies, the presidency—nay— the very existence of George W. Bush.' The first use of the term 'Trump derangement syndrome' may have been by Esther Goldberg in an August 2015 op-ed in *The American Spectator*; she applied the term to 'Ruling Class Republicans' who are dismissive or contemptuous of Trump. Krauthammer, in an op-ed criticizing Trump, commented that—in addition to general hysteria about Trump—the 'Trump Derangement Syndrome' was the 'inability to distinguish between legitimate policy differences and signs of psychic pathology' in his behavior." —Wikipedia

The logical, conservative, traditional right focuses on Trump's policies and accomplishments while the emotional, liberal, progressive left focuses on his pathologies and personality. Dennis Prager's ten points mentioned earlier perfectly explain why. The left prefers an articulate sensitive man like Obama who makes them feel good, while the right prefers a confident aggressive man like Trump who gets the job done. Obama was a kiss-ass-play-games politician; Trump is a kick-ass-take-names businessman.

TDS is the acute onset of paranoia in otherwise normal people in reaction to the policies, the presidency—nay—the very existence of Donald J. Trump.

CHAPTER 3
DEMOCRATS, SOCIALISTS, COMMUNISTS

If I had published what I know about the Democratic party and its association with communism several decades ago ... or even a few years ago, I would have sounded liked a right-wing nut job, a McCarthyite, to most ordinary Americans. But after two terms of a young communist sympathizer as president, an old communist hippie running for president as a democratic socialist, and Obama's VP, Quid Pro Joe, leading the pack in the democrat primary, it does not sound so out there anymore.

The facts in this book are all now in the public domain, but connecting the dots requires research and deductive reasoning. J. Edgar Hoover knew all about the communist threat, but his private files were destroyed when he died, per his instructions ... I do not know why. He may have decided he knew too much about too many. Perhaps he did not want to disclose his sources and methods. Perhaps he knew his methods were extra-constitutional. Who knows?

What we do know is that Hoover and his agents watched and documented the communist infiltration of our government, Hollywood, academia, the media, churches, and even the Manhattan Project for forty-eight years as Director of Intelligence in 1924, and then Director of the Federal Bureau of Investigation, which he started, from 1935 until his death in 1972.

Hoover and his bureau took down many Soviet spy rings over those years, but he could not stop many of their goals for the destruction of America from the inside from being achieved because many Americans had drunk the Kool-Aid, becoming communist sympathizers themselves, and one of the political parties had been "captured" ... the one Reagan left when he realized it.

We all know Bernie is a socialist, but I have been asked, "Was Obama also a socialist, and would Biden follow in his footsteps?" Without labels, just look at what they stand for and desire to impose on us—Obamacare, welfare growth, open borders, sanctuary cities, regulation expansion, higher taxes, depleted military, politicizing and weaponizing the FBI, CIA, NSA, EPA, IRS, Pentagon, Medicare-for-all, Green New Deal, Paris Climate Accord, Iran Nuke Deal, War-on-Coal, Oil, Natural Gas, Nuclear, Student loan forgiveness, free college tuition, historical revisionism, suppression of conservative free speech, liberal dominance of university tenured positions, rejection of school choice, unionism, fake news, entertainment bias, gun control/confiscation, etc. are all socialist ideas and just the tip of the iceberg for the democrat socialist agenda for America. So, yes,—Obama is a Marxist-inspired socialist, and yes—Biden is an Obama-inspired socialist.

Compare them with Trump's conservative policies and positions—lower taxes, reduced regulations, stronger military, booming economy, record stock market, return of manufacturing jobs, higher wages, closed borders to illegals, banning sanctuary cities, curbing EPA's radical agenda, withdrawing from the disastrous Iran Nuke Deal and Paris Climate Accord, putting China, North Korea, Russia on notice, bankrupting or destroying Iran, holding deep state operatives accountable, encouraging energy production for energy independence, school choice, free speech for all, etc.

The difference between a liberal socialist agenda and a conservative free-market agenda could not be more stark in 2020.

Acquiring centralized control of the means of production and distribution of products and services by expanding the jurisdiction of the government over all aspects of citizen's communal and private lives is the very definition of socialism, whether it happens through legislation and executive action like in America and Europe or bloody revolution like in Cuba, Venezuela, Russia, and China.

Communists typically advocate bloody revolution, socialists in a democracy conspiratorial evolution. Communist leaders lie and commit murder to acquire their power; democratic socialists lie and commit fraud to acquire their power. The results are the same for the losers … loss of life, liberty, and the pursuit of happiness resulting ultimately in mutually shared poverty and tyranny for the masses, riches and power for the elites.

My research is a compilation of information from dozens of books by serious conservative authors like Newt Gingrich, David Horowitz, Dinesh D'souza, Mark Levin, Victor David Hanson, and several communist authors like Karl Marx and Saul Alinsky. A complete bibliography and comments on each book are in the appendix.

The statements made regarding people, ideology, history, and activities are based in facts and the much-acknowledged research and experience of others, not just my opinion … although some deductive reasoning was required to connect the dots.

Connecting the dots was what our intelligence agencies failed to do prior to 9/11. If democrats prevail in 2020, I believe the impact on America will be more catastrophic and long-lasting than 9/11. The fact patterns I am presenting here portend potential disaster for America in 2020. Vote wisely in November!

CHAPTER 4
SOROS AND SANDERS

Although he keeps a low profile, George Soros is one of the key puppet masters of the modern socialist movement, organizing and coordinating various activists' groups, supporting counterculture rebellions, and pulling together billions of dollars to subvert and defeat conservatives and their values across the world. *The Shadow Party*, a 2006 book by David Horowitz, a reformed communist, describes Soros' activities in some detail. There really is a vast left-wing conspiracy, and George Soros has been its puppet master for decades. In 2005, Byron York wrote a book named *The Vast Left-Wing Conspiracy: The Untold Story of How Democratic Operatives, Eccentric Billionaires, Liberal Activists, and Assorted Celebrities Tried to Bring Down a President – and Why They'll Try Even Harder Next Time.*

David Horowitz and Byron York report the following about Soros. On July 13, 2003, a cabal of political strategists, wealthy donors, left-wing labor leaders, and other democrat activists gathered at the Soros mansion on Long Island. Previously the McCain-Feingold act, which Soros vigorously supported, had limited soft money contributions to political candidates and parties and severely limited hard money contributions also. This had a crippling impact on the ability of democrats to raise big money from unions, Hollywood studios, trial lawyers, and other large donor sources but not much impact on republican fundraising which was typically small amounts from each of millions of donors.

So why did Soros back this bill since he hates republicans and backs left-wing democrat candidates? John McCain and Russ Feingold played right into his hands. By drying up democrat sources, Soros could create an alternative that he controlled, and when you control the money you control the party. Now they would need a new scheme, and Soros was prepared to offer them one.

Invitees to this confab were big money liberal icons. You may recognize some of these names. These names are present in various public documents.

- Morton H. Halperin, a veteran political culture warrior, who Soros had hired the previous year to head his Open Society Institute in Washington

- John Podesta, a lawyer whose political career began in 1972, when he worked for George McGovern's unsuccessful presidential campaign. He also served in the Clinton and Obama Administration. He started a liberal think tank, Center for American Progress. Podesta is the archetypical liberal. Remember him from the Clinton campaign of 2016; it was his emails that were hacked. It was reported that his password was "password"

- Robert Rubin, Clinton's Treasury Secretary

- Steven Rosenthal, a left-wing union leader, advisor to Robert Reich

- Carl Pope, executive director of the Sierra Club

- Ellen Malcolm, founder, and president of Emily's List

- Peter B. Lewis, CEO of Progressive Insurance and many others of their ilk.

It is reported that a new organization began to emerge, and Mr. Soros pledged $10 million to get it started. With Soros's pledge the money flowed into an existing liberal activist group called America Coming Together (ACT) that had not gotten off the ground, languishing for donors. This group would now coordinate the activities of the new "Shadow Party." They would sponsor get-out-the-vote drives, combining the efforts of left-wing unions, radical environmentalists, abortion-rights groups, and race warriors from various civil rights groups like the NAACP.

Initially they used a dodge known as "527," a chapter in the IRS code that allowed untraceable donations of any amount. After the feds got on to that scam, they now use 501(c)(4), tax exempt nonprofit. Money flows into the 501(c)(4) then out to nonpartisan causes, right?

> "A **527**-organization or **527 group** is a type of U.S. tax-exempt organization organized under Section **527** of the U.S. Internal Revenue Code (26 U.S.C. § **527**). A **527 group** is created primarily to influence the selection, nomination, election, appointment, or defeat of candidates to federal, state, or local public office."
> —Wikipedia

> "A 501(c)(4) is a **nonprofit organization that is capable of extensive lobbying activities**, as opposed to a 501(c)(3), which is setup for charitable giving and extremely limited in the amount of political lobbying it can do. Foundation owners are only required to distribute around 10 percent or less directly to charities and causes, depending on how they are set up, the remainder is available for expenses and salaries." —Wikipedia

When a foundation pockets most of its contributions for the owners and their friends it could be considered a legal money laundering scheme. The Clinton Foundation, said to be one of the world's most successful, for the Clintons, is a 501(c)(3).

The following are a few of the members of the America Votes coalition founded and coordinated by the Shadow Party of George Soros. These are all liberal organizations associated with George Soros, international socialists.

- ACORN (Association of Community Organizations for Reform Now)

- ACT (America Coming Together)

- AFL–CIO (huge labor union)

- AFSCME (American Federation of State, County, and Municipal Employees)

- AFT (American Federation of Teachers union)

- NEA (National Education Association teacher's union)

- ATLA (Association of Trial Lawyers of America)

- EMILY'S List (pro-abortion women's political advocacy group)

- League of Conservation Voters

- NAACP (National Association for the Advancement of Colored Politicians)

- NARAL Pro-Choice America (abortion advocacy group)

- National Jewish Democratic Council

- National Treasury Employees Union

- People for the American Way

- Planned Parenthood Action Fund

- Service Employees International Union (SEIU—a far left union)

- Sierra Club

- Young Voters Alliance

Soros, one of the world's most financially successful capitalist uses his capital to plot the defeat of capitalism, which he hates with a passion only a fellow socialist like Bernie Sanders could appreciate. Soros' self-stated goal is to bring down all the world's institutions and replace them with a new world order he describes as an Open Society … a classless, borderless, god-free, gun-free, socialist, stateless utopia run by someone like him!

By comparison, Bernie is just an old Woodstock-era Vermont hippie turned communist in his 20s who has lived off the government and his girlfriends/wives his entire adult life. He never held a real job, made a productive living, provided jobs or payroll to anyone, invented anything, produced anything, or as much as managed a lemonade stand. He is all talk, no action but his constant blathering has resonated with millions of disgruntled Americans who, like him, prefer free stuff to freedom—a simple definition of socialism. Lincoln had another good one, "you work, I eat." Of course, Lincoln was talking about slavery, but then so is Sanders. All those preferring free stuff to freedom are democrats, or worse!

Bernie has never held any real political power or passed any significant legislation, but he would like to. As president it is difficult to even imagine the damage President Sanders could do to America just with executive action, cabinet and bureaucratic appointments, and deep state resources ... not to mention the power of being the Commander-in-Chief. The thought of President Biden, aka Obama 3.0, aka quid pro Joe, sleepy/creepy/demented Joe is no more comforting!

Bernie sees himself as a Robin Hoodesque character righting wrongs, taking from the rich, giving to the poor. He is still the same commie-type hippie he was sixty years ago. He is consistent if nothing else. All Bernie's fans are democrats, or worse ... much worse! And yet, Bernie won the first three democrat primaries, Iowa, New Hampshire, and a landslide victory in Nevada. Even though at the time of this writing Bernie will not likely be the nominee, he and his supporters, typified by AOC and 40+ percent of democrat voters, are not going anywhere. Young people are especially loyal to Bernie because his message of free stuff and social justice appeals to naïve youth who have no historical knowledge of what communism or socialism means ... and their minds have been plied by liberal teachers and professors for decades, exactly as the Goal # 17 intended...

> "Get control of the schools. Use them as transmission belts
> for socialism and current Communist propaganda. Soften
> the curriculum. Get control of teachers' associations. Put
> the party line in textbooks."

Obama, Biden, and Sanders have all vowed to "fundamentally transform" America in TV interviews. Since Obama first pronounced it a few days before his first election, "transform America" has become a prominent theme of the socialist democrat party. Do not be deceived, these liberals are all on the same page when it comes to America's future direction.

Bloomberg may be more pragmatic than Sanders and Warren, but he is a gun-grabber, climate change fanatic, and a control freak, i.e., a socialist in capitalists clothing. Bloomberg, having dropped out, is pledging his considerable organization and unlimited funds to defeat President Trump, like Soros did to defeat Bush in 2004. Soros, Sanders, Biden, Obama, Clinton, Warren, and Bloomberg represent an existential threat to traditional American values, and they will all be backing Obama 3.0, Quid Pro Joe Biden, when the dust settles. All leftist progressives are democrats or worse!

CHAPTER 5
THE NAKED COMMUNIST EPIPHANY

I first became politically minded around 1975 when I read *The Naked Communist* and found out the old Soviet communists' plan for the destruction of America from the inside matched up closely with the positions, tactics, and strategies of the national democrat party. As a scientist/engineer I applied analytical thinking, deductive reasoning, and mathematical logic to the subject of politics, current events, and world and American history. I have never voted for a democrat for any position—fed, state, or local since.

My conclusion was that while not all democrats were communists or socialists, all subversive communists, socialists, and their sympathizer comrades in America were democrats, gangsters, or worse, and they had made tremendous progress undermining, subverting, infiltrating, and corrupting America since the early twentieth century. They had setbacks like Joe McCarthy's communist inquisition in the 50s but reemerged in the 60s and 70s, then another setback when anti-communist Reagan was elected in 1980. Two steps forward, one step back … progress delayed, but not denied. In 2020, committed socialist like Soros, Sanders, Obama, and their ilk are circling the wagons to prevent President Trump from defeating them again and putting them on the reservation for another four years or longer.

Obama inspired all young communist sympathizers in America to up their game and come out of the closet, but then Trump shot them down again. An emboldened left is now running and winning with openly socialist candidates who express contempt for traditional American values. All progressives are democrats or worse!

The culmination of this cabal's power grab in the last century may have been when JFK was assassinated in 1963. Lee Harvey Oswald *may* have pulled the trigger, but there is no way he pulled off John F. Kennedy's (JFK) assassination alone, my opinion anyway. Jack Ruby, a mob figure, had likely already made a deal with the conspirators to eliminate Oswald before Kennedy even arrived in Dallas.

The man who said, "Ask not what your country can do for you, but what you can do for your country," was gone and replaced by Lyndon B. Johnson (LBJ), who said, "Ask what your country can do for you; your wish is my command … as long as we have your votes." How convenient for the communists, the mob, the Democratic Party, and certain black civil rights leaders. Another assassination, in 1968, of Dr. Martin Luther King Jr., eliminated a champion of peace and love politics, which was not what the commies, democrats, or Soros needed to keep race relations inflamed. Again, how convenient. A few months later, JFK's brother Bobby, a mob-hating crime fighter as Attorney General, was also eliminated as he ran for president. Watch your back Trump!

Woodstock, a music festival drawing four hundred thousand people to Bernie's Vermont neighborhood in August 1969, became a defining event for the counterculture generation. Communists saw this as fertile recruiting ground for future revolutionaries and "useful idiots," Lenin and Stalin's name for their admirers in the American press, movies, academia, and government.

While the counterculture hippies, commies, draft dodgers, dopers, dead-heads, and do-gooders like Bernie and his girlfriends were doing their thing, I was saving the planet cleaning up the last generation's industrial pollution, a young Donald J. Trump, having graduated from the Wharton School of Business in 1968, was building his portfolio of Manhattan real estate, a young lawyer Joe Biden was preparing to run for the U.S. Senate, and Saul Alinsky was putting the final touches on his classic *Rules for Radicals*, published in 1971. That same year Barry Soetoro, aka Barack Hussein Obama, returned from living four years in a Muslim country, Indonesia, to live with his grandparents in Honolulu, under the influence of the old communist Frank Marshall Davis, a friend of his grandfather, and some say his biological father. Yep, those were the days! Fifty years ago, no one could have imagined what America and the world would look like in 2020.

LBJ's reign in the Whitehouse at the height of the Vietnam War was a turning point in American history for lots of reasons. Related to the subject of this book, he was the king of free stuff and could arguably be labeled the first postwar Socialist president. Democrats see welfare as buying votes and border control as voter suppression. Johnson was a real pro at this. He consolidated the black vote for democrats by "giving them something, but not too much" in his Great Society programs. It was the beginning of an era of dependency Johnson predicted would enslave blacks to the Democratic party and free stuff for two hundred years. Democrats were the party of slavery and the KKK, now they are the party of socialism, Black Lies Matter, and Antifa. LBJ deserves a lot of the credit for facilitating that transformation.

Since Jimmy Carter flung upon Florida's borders to Cubans escaping Castro's regime and subsequently mandated bilingual education for all, democrats have done everything possible, legal and illegal, to increase the influx from south of the border and secure the Hispanic-voting bloc, like they did the blacks in Johnson's day. Free stuff is a powerful draw to people who have little … stuff or freedom!

I believe both power grabs were premeditated democrat schemes to secure votes without concern for the harm to individuals, families, women, or children they impacted, especially American citizens. Burgess Owens, famous former NFL player and author, recently told Congress that the democrats owe his people reparations for the cultural genocide of the black family and community their policies had produced.

It took considerable planning, plotting, scheming, manipulating, cajoling, and bribing to subjugate Blacks and Hispanics. Both these groups were traditionally religious, family-oriented, conservative cultures. Their new Massa's on the other hand are generally irreligious, pro-abortion, socialist, liberal, white politicians. The "Uncle Toms," like Al Sharpton and Jesse Jackson, in the democratic party, participated profitably in the decimation of the black family and community by the democrat's welfare state programs. They, like members of the Congressional Black Caucus today, sold out their principles and became professional racists shilling for white democrats. These are the same democrats who want to take over every area of our lives in 2020 and beyond … that is what socialists do!

All welfare state and illegal immigration advocates are democrats, or worse! Trump is replacing the welfare state with an opportunity state and building a wall to keep illegals out … and it is working, especially for poor blacks and legal Hispanics, but not for democrat politicians.

THE MOST DESTRUCTIVE PEOPLE IN AMERICA IN THE LAST EIGHTY YEARS

BY Frank Hawkins, who was a captain in Army Intelligence, serving as a case officer in clandestine collection operations for the Defense Intelligence Agency during the Cold War in Germany.

"America has undergone enormous change during the nearly eight decades of my life.

Today, America is a bitterly divided, poorly educated, and morally fragile society with so-called mainstream politicians pushing cynical identity politics, socialism, and open borders. The president of the United States has been threatened with impeachment because the other side doesn't like him. The once reasonably unbiased American media has evolved into a hysterical left-wing mob.

How could the stable and reasonably cohesive America of the 1950s have reached this point in just one lifetime? Who are the main culprits? Here's my list of the ten most destructive Americans of the last eighty years.

10. Mark Felt: Deputy director of the FBI, aka "Deep Throat" during the Watergate scandal. This was the first public instance of a senior FBI official directly interfering in America's political affairs. He was the forerunner of James Comey, Peter Strzok, Lisa Page, and Andrew McCabe.

9. Bill Ayers: He represents the deep and ongoing leftist ideological damage to our education system is an unrepentant American terrorist who evaded punishment, and devoted his career to radicalizing American education and pushing leftist causes. Ghost wrote Obama's book, "Dreams from My Father."

8. Teddy Kennedy: Most folks remember Teddy as the guy who left Mary Jo Kopechne to die in his submerged car at Chappaquiddick. The real damage came after he avoided punishment for her death and became a major democratic force in the U.S. Senate, pushing through transformative liberal policies in health care and education. The most consequential was the 1965 Hart–Cellar immigration bill he pushed hard for that changed the quota system to increase the flow of third

world people without skills into the U.S. and essentially ended large-scale immigration from Europe.

7. Walter Cronkite: Cronkite was a much beloved network anchor who began the politicization of America's news media with his infamous broadcast from Vietnam that described the Tet Offensive as a major victory for the communists and significantly turned the gullible American public against the Vietnam War. In fact, the Tet Offensive was a military disaster for the North Vietnamese Army (NVA) and Viet Cong, later admitted by North Vietnamese military leaders. Decades later Cronkite admitted he got the story wrong. But it was too late. The damage was done.

6. Bill and Hillary Clinton: It's difficult to separate Team Clinton. Bill's presidency was largely benign as he was a relative fiscal conservative who rode the remaining benefits of the Reagan Era. But his sexual exploits badly stained the Oval Office and negatively affected America's perception of the presidency. In exchange for financial support, he facilitated the transfer of sensitive military technology to the Chinese. Hillary, a Saul Alinsky acolyte, is one of the most vicious politicians of my lifetime, covering up Bill's sexual assaults by harassing and insulting the exploited women and peddling influence around the globe in exchange for funds for the corrupt Clinton Foundation. She signed off on the sale of 20 percent of the U.S. uranium reserve to the Russians after Bill received a $500,000 speaking fee in Moscow and the foundation (which supported the Clinton's regal lifestyle) received hundreds of millions of dollars from those who benefited from the

deal. Between them they killed any honor that might have existed in the dark halls of DC.

5. Valerie Jarrett: The Rasputin of the Obama administration. A red diaper baby, her father, maternal grandfather, and father-in-law (Vernon Jarrett who was a close friend and ally of Obama's mentor Frank Marshall Davis) were hardcore communists under investigation by the U.S. government. She has been chirping in Obama's ear for his entire political career pushing a strong anti-American, Islamist, anti-Israeli, socialist/communist, cling-to-power agenda.

4. Jimmy Carter: Carter ignited modern day radical Islam by abandoning the Shah and paving the way for Ayatollah Khomeini to take power in Tehran. Iran subsequently became the main state sponsor and promoter of international Islamic terrorism. When Islamists took over our embassy in Tehran, Carter was too weak to effectively respond, thus strengthening the rule of the radical Islamic mullahs. *(Carter also gave us double digit inflation, 18* percent *mortgage rates, and an energy shortage he admonished us was permanent. "Get used to it," he had said.)*

3. Lyndon Johnson: Johnson turned the Vietnam conflict into a major war for America. It could have ended early if he had listened to the generals instead of automaker Robert McNamara. The ultimate result was:

    A. Fifty-eight thousand American military deaths and collaterally tens of thousands of American lives damaged; and

B. A war that badly divided America and created left-wing groups that evaded the draft and eventually gained control of our education system.

Even worse, his so-called War on Poverty led to the destruction of American black families with a significant escalation of welfare and policies designed to keep poor families dependent on the government (and voting democrat) for their well-being. He deliberately created a racial holocaust that is still burning today. A strong case could be made for putting him at the top of this list.

2. Barack Hussein Obama: He set up America for a final defeat and stealth conversion from a free market society to socialism/communism. As we get deeper into the Trump presidency, we learn more each day about how Obama politicized and compromised key government agencies, most prominently the FBI, the CIA, and the IRS, thus thoroughly shaking the public's confidence in the federal government to be fair and unbiased in its activities. He significantly set back race and other relations between Americans by stoking black grievances and pushing radical identity politics. Obama's open support for the Iranian mullahs and his apologetic "lead from behind" foreign policy seriously weakened America abroad. His blatant attempt to interfere in Israel's election trying to unseat Netanyahu is one of the most shameful things ever done by an American president.

The Number One Worst American is John Kerry. Some readers will likely say Kerry does not deserve to be number one on this list. I have him here because I regard him as the most despicable American who ever lived. After his three faked purple hearts during his cowardly service in Vietnam, he was able to leave the U.S. Navy early. As a reserve naval officer and in clear violation of the Uniform Code of Military Justice, he traveled to Paris and met privately with the NVA and the Viet Cong. He returned to the United States parroting the Soviet party line about the war and testified before Congress comparing American soldiers to the hordes of Genghis Khan. It was a clear case of treason, giving aid and comfort to the enemy in a time of war. We got a second bite of the bitter Kerry apple when, as Obama's secretary of state, he fell into bed with the Iranian ("Death to America") mullahs giving them the ultimate green light to develop nuclear weapons along with billions of dollars that further supported their terrorist activities. Only the heroic Swift Boat Vets saved us from a Manchurian Candidate Kerry presidency. Ultimately, we got Obama.

Dishonorable Mentions! (People who just missed the list)

John Brennan: Obama's CIA director who once voted for communist Gus Hall for president. A key member of the deep state who severely politicized the CIA and called President Trump treasonous for meeting with the president of Russia.

Jane Fonda: The movie actress who made the infamous trip to Vietnam during the war in support of the communists. She represents hard left Hollywood that has done so much damage to our culture.

Jimmy Hendrix and Janice Joplin: Both revered entertainers helped usher in the prevailing drug culture and personally suffered the consequences. Karma's a bitch.

Robert Johnson: As head of BET, he helped popularize ho's, bitches, and pimps while making millions on great hits such as "Jigga my Nigga," "Big Pimpin," "Niggas in Paris," and "Strictly 4 My N.I.G.G.A.Z." Many scholars within the African American community maintain that BET perpetuates and justifies racism by adopting the stereotypes held about African Americans, affecting the psyche of young viewers through the bombardment of negative images of African Americans. Who can disagree?

Arthur Ochs Sulzberger, Jr.: He is the head of *the New York Times*. Once the gold standard of American journalism, the paper always had a liberal tilt and occasionally made bad mistakes. As the years have gone along, the paper has slid further and further left and today it is virtually the primary propaganda arm of the increasingly radical Democratic Party. It still retains influence in Washington and New York.

Frank Marshall Davis: He is the anti-white, black Bolshevik, card-carrying Soviet agent. Also, he is the probable birth father and admitted primary mentor of young Barack Hussein Obama.

George Soros: A special reward goes to him. Jewish former Nazi collaborator in his native Hungary who as a self-made billionaire has poured hundreds of millions of dollars into left-wing groups and causes. The damage he has caused is difficult to measure, but it is certainly large. He has funded much of the effort to destroy the Trump presidency."

Most names on this list are either prominent DEMOCRATS or allied with them. I could add one who is not, or was not at the time…

George W. Bush who, after 9/11 failed to wipe out the Taliban, terminate Osama Bin Laden and Al Qaeda, but then invaded Iraq to take out Iran's worst nightmare, Iraq's leader Saddam Hussein based on flawed intelligence, and cost America trillions of dollars, thousands of lives, many more thousands of young American's maimed for life in what would become America's longest war. With Saddam gone, Iran was free to pursue its terrorist conquest of the middle east and death threats to America and Israel. GW and his father GHW Bush are example of institutional Republicans who along with their counterparts in the Democrat Party brought us higher taxes, more federal involvement in education and welfare, the largest national debt in history, a depleted military, offshoring of millions of jobs, Chinese expansionism and theft of our intellectual property...and, oh yeah - the financial crisis and recession of 2008. Trump calls them all "stupid politicians." When you oversee America as President and Commander in Chief, stupid is dangerous. When it comes to negative long-term consequences of poor choices and decisions, GW Bush is right down there with the worst...Obama, Carter, and LBJ.

On the other hand, in just 3 years Trump destroyed the ISIS Caliphate Obama precipitated , killed Iran's top general Suleiman, enforced a red line with Syria, moved Israel's capital to Jerusalem, brought back manufacturing jobs, made NATO countries pay their fair share, put China, North Korea, and Russia in their place, generated a record stock market and unemployment rate, and so much more...not brilliant, just not stupid!

CHAPTER 6
ALINSKY'S RULES FOR RADICALS AND SUN-TSE'S ART OF WAR

The other book that profoundly influenced my thinking was Saul Alinsky's *Rules for Radicals*. Alinsky was an American communist who survived the "McCarthy holocaust" as he put it to realize a different approach was needed … subversion and infiltration in the 70s rather than violent confrontation of the 60s He wrote what became the new-left's playbook which both Hillary and Obama used to guide their progress toward real political power. All "new-left" activists are democrats, or worse!

I will repeatedly use the theme from Saul Alinsky's book *Rules for Radicals*, 1971… how to transform America from what it is to what they believe it should be. What is wrong with that you may say, isn't that what the American colonists did in 1776? I'll juxtapose communism with Americanism in a later chapter. Alinsky and his followers helped infiltrate and take over the democrat party after 1968, as their Soviet communist mentors advised them to do.

Alinsky, an old-school communist, developed the new left's "community organizer" model that would inspire a young Hillary Clinton and later an articulate young black man Barack Obama. Remember his words, "…we will fundamentally transform America." All Alinsky followers including ACORN, Planned Parenthood, Obama, Clinton, and many others are democrats, or worse!

Alinsky proposed ten rules or tactics for how the have-nots can take power away from the haves. But, the first principle of radical change is to motivate the change agents to see their grievances, target their oppressors, and develop a rational pragmatic plan of action. In 2020 Black Lives Matter, with help from the Democrat Party's propaganda arm the fake-news media, have convinced a large segment of white America they are guilty of systemic racism and deserve whatever violence is thrown at them because whites are the villains and blacks are the victims. Although this assertion defies rational analysis, whites in authority have capitulated to their demands, even allowing anarchist to take over portions of American cities in the name of social justice. Alinsky would be proud of them but advise them to take another more subtle approach. The generation of radicals in the 60s acted out with riots, bombings, marches, and confrontations. They were put down by authorities, like anarchists should be. In 2020 Antifa is a classic example of anarchy and how not to get what you want, although in sympathetic democrat states they seem to act pretty much with impunity. Even more devastating to their causes in the '60's was that the moral and silent majority of mostly white Americans rejected them and their message of revolution and in 1968 rejected their democrat candidate for president, Hubert Humphrey, for Richard Nixon in an electoral landslide. I believe we will see history repeat itself in 2020. I believe, once again, a moral and silent majority of patriotic law-abiding religious Americans are seething with anger and disdain on the inside just waiting for the November elections. Alinsky noted this predictable rejection and admonished his followers to pursue a new path, one of infiltration of the system and working from within for change. But he recognized that even if a comrade is on the inside, pressure is still needed from the outside. His *Rules for Radicals, A Pragmatic Primer for Realistic Radicals* addressed both.

It is beyond the scope of this book to discuss and give examples for each of these rules.

Suffice it to say, Alinsky was a brilliant man and his book is an excellent and succinct read. Marx may have codified the principals of communism and socialism, but Alinsky wrote the pragmatic rules for achieving their goals in America in the 60s and beyond. He was the first "community organizer," and his tactics are still the gold standard for the left ... and, in fact, I can see a lot of Donald Trump's *The Art of the Deal* in these tactics—how he manipulates the press, ridicules opponents, creates leverage, makes deals, and confounds democrats (the enemy)! Psychological warfare tactics can be applied by the right or the left because human nature is the same for all, and never changes, even over the centuries.

Democrats want to fundamentally transform America (Obama's words) from what it is—a conservative, god-trusting, gun-owing, pro-life, free enterprise, capitalistic republic where individual liberty, the pursuit of happiness, and justice for all are supreme ... to what they believe it should be—a liberal, godless, gun-free, pro-abortion, centrally regulated, socialist bureaucracy where collective submission, radical egalitarianism, and justice for elites only are supreme ... liberals call this social justice, but history says otherwise. They still use Alinsky's tactics so it is important for conservative politicians to understand them.

The new left playbook was written in 1971 by Saul Alinsky but his ideas were almost twenty-five hundred years old. I feel certain that Alinsky knew of Sun-Tse's tactics.

Excerpts from *The Art of War* by Sun-Tse are mentioned ahead. A few of the forty-five communist goals from *The Naked Communist* are inserted for comparison. Bet you didn't know the left, all democrats, has been running a twenty-five-hundred-year-old game plan on America since the early twentieth century!

About five hundred years before Christ, Chinese warrior Sun-Tse laid out the rules for political and psychological subversion. He was thinking of wars between countries and civilizations but a lot of what is going on today is applicable.

Alinsky's *Rules for Radicals* and the forty-five communist goals for the destruction of America from the inside can easily be seen in context of *The Art of War* ... they are all about political and psychological warfare. The new left of Obama, Clinton, Biden, Bernie, Warren, Pelosi, Schumer, and Schiff are masters of these tactics ... but Trump is the grand master!

> *"There is no higher art than that of destroying the enemy resistance without a fight on the battlefield. The direct tactic of war is necessary only on the battlefield; but only the indirect tactic can lead to a real and lasting victory."*
> —The Art of War

> *"Subvert anything of value in the enemy's country. Implicate the emissaries of the major powers in criminal undertakings; undermine their positions and destroy their reputation in other ways as well and expose them to public ridicule of their fellow citizens."*
> —The Art of War

Goals of communism:

- *Continue discrediting American culture by degrading all forms of artistic expression. An American communist cell was told to "eliminate all good sculpture from parks and building, substitute shapeless, awkward, and meaningless forms."*

- *Control art critics and directors of art museums. "Our plan is to promote ugliness, repulsive meaningless art."*

- *Eliminate all laws governing obscenity by calling them "censorship" and a violation of free speech and free press.*

- *Breakdown cultural standard of morality by promoting pornography and obscenity in books, magazines, motion pictures, radio, and TV.*

- *Present homosexuality, degeneracy, and promiscuity as "normal, natural, and healthy."*

- *Discredit the American Constitution by calling it inadequate, old-fashioned, out of step with modern needs, a hindrance to cooperation between nations on a world-wide basis.*

- *Discredit the American founding fathers. Present them as selfish aristocrats who had no concern for the "common man."*

- *Belittle all forms of American culture and discourage the teaching of American history on the ground that it was only a minor part of "the big picture." Give more emphasis to Russian history since the communists took over.*

- *Discredit and eventually dismantle the FBI*

- *Infiltrate and gain control of more unions.*

- *Infiltrate and gain control of big business.*

"Do not shun the aid of even the lowest and most despicable people. Disrupt the work of their government with every means you can." —The Art of War

Goals of communism:

- *Promote the U.N. as the only hope for mankind. If its charter is rewritten, demand that it is set up as one-world government with its own independent armed forces.*

- *Resist any attempt to outlaw the Communist Party.*

- *Do away with all loyalty oaths.*

- *Capture one or both political parties in the United States.*

- *Use technical decisions of the courts to weaken basic American institutions by claiming their activities violate rights.*

"Spread disunity and dispute among the citizens of the enemy's territory. Turn the young against the old. Use every means to destroy their arms, their supplies, and the discipline of the enemy's forces. Debase old traditions and accepted gods. Be generous with promises and rewards to purchase intelligence and accomplices. Send out your secret agents in all directions. Do not skimp with money or promises, for their yield high return." —The Art of War

Goals of Communism:

- *Infiltrate the churches and replace revealed religion with "social" religion. Discredit the Bible and emphasize the need for intellectual maturity which does not need a "religious crutch."*

- *Eliminate prayer or any phase of religious expression in the schools on the grounds that it violates the principle of "separation of church and state."*

- *Support any socialist movement to give centralized control over any part of the culture—education, social agencies, welfare programs, mental health clinics, etc.*

- *Get control of the schools. Use them as transmission belts for socialism and current Communist propaganda. Soften the curriculum. Get control of teachers' associations. Put the party line in textbooks.*

- *Gain control of all student newspapers.*

- *Use student riots to foment public protests against programs or organizations which are under communist attack.*

- *Infiltrate the press. Get control of book-review assignments, editorial writing, and policy-making positions.*

- *Gain control of key positions in radio, TV, and pictures*

Do these tactics and goals sound familiar? They should if you are paying attention.

The Art of War is a well-known text at every war college in the world. It is also taught in many business schools' executive training, which is where I was introduced to it. Trump's *Art of the Deal* is his version of Sun-Tse 's *Art of War!*

CHAPTER 7
WHAT DO SOCIALISTS REALLY WANT?

Liberals/socialists want control over every aspect of our lives, including health care, education, environment, industry, immigration, military, and law enforcement. They came within one close election of capturing the country in 2016. The reign of Hillary the Hun and her minions inside and outside government would have ended America as we have known it for a generation at least. These folks are all democrats, or worse!

Over the last several decades socialism, once an unthinkable evil associated with Soviet communism, has been normalized by democrat party operatives, eccentric billionaires like George Soros, politicians like Barak Obama, liberal activists, assorted celebrities, the main stream media, university academia and administrations, wealthy elites in government, industry, law, arts, and entertainment. This group are all democrats, or worse!

Each advocacy group has its own specific interests, but it shares a common Marxist worldview that "all the world's struggles have been, and still are, "class struggles" i.e., between the haves and the have-nots. Today's liberals include a long list of victim classes versus villain classes such as blacks versus whites, gays versus straights, poor versus rich, old versus young, illiterate versus educated, illegal criminals versus ICE, undocumented immigrants versus citizens, females versus males, climate change believers versus deniers, atheists versus Christians, everyone versus republicans, etc. This is the very essence of "identity politics," i.e., pitting one group against another to dupe the voters and force societal change.

Not so coincidently this was Karl Marx's main theme when writing the *Communist Manifesto* in 1848. Now, some see this as an opportunity to take control, some to make huge sums of money, others to save the planet, others to establish social justice, and Soros to create a classless, borderless, stateless, god-free, gun-free, utopia, he calls an Open Society.

Regardless of motivation, all socialist movements, throughout history, have sought to fundamentally transform society from it is to what they believe it should be ... a utopia where social justice prevails, or else! Some would do this through bloody revolution, others through bloodless evolution. So far America is the latter ... so far! I assert that democrats in 2020 are inextricably linked through their ideology and heritage to Karl Marx and far left communism and socialism. Communists and socialists in America are all democrats.

Recent polls show that most of our young adults called millennials now prefer socialism over free-enterprise capitalism. Hence, unless something changes soon, socialist politicians are one generation away from fundamentally transforming America, from what it is ... a religious, pro-life, gun-owning, conservative, free-enterprise, equal opportunity, law abiding, prosperous, safe, sovereign, constitutional republic (Trump's America) to what they believe it should be ... a god-free, gun-free, pro-abortion, liberal, classless, borderless, lawless, illegal-sanctuary, corrupt socialist partocracy (democrat's Amerika) where the productive class, entrepreneurs, business owners ,and hard workers are highly taxed and regulated to produce equal outcomes for the less productive classes.

While socialism may sound fair and compassionate to some, all of human history shows that when any large group of humans living together is forced into an order dictated by a domineering central government, even if with benevolent, good intent at first, the strongest among them always eventually takes control and individual freedom of the masses is lost. Juxtapose that with a country established by the free will of men and women operating under a decentralized hamstrung government of the people, by the people, and for the people, like the United States of America. Conservatives do not want large efficient government, we want as little government as possible, making it as difficult as possible for them to increase their control over our lives, and this is what the founders meant for the Constitution to do. This may be why liberals/socialists disregard the constitution as written and intended.

Justice Neal Gorsuch said during his confirmation process, "Conservatives just want to be left alone to live their lives as they see fit, within the Constitution and the Law." Trump's strategy was simple ... unleash the immense potential of the American people—get the government out of the way, out of their pockets, off their backs ... and watch what happens. What happened was job growth, increased salaries, manufacturing returned to America, small businesses expanded, labor participation improved, food stamps decreased, etc. Not brilliant, just not stupid ... like his predecessors.

The History of Modern Socialism in Post-War America

After having survived the anti-communist holocaust of McCarthyism and the take down of spy rings by J. Edgar Hoover's FBI in the 50s, the left took a nasty turn toward violence in the 60s—Viet Nam war protests, riots in Berkeley and Watts, police killings, and the disastrous 1968 Democratic Convention in Chicago. The convention was held during a year of violence, political turbulence, and civil unrest, particularly riots in more than a hundred cities following the assassination of Martin Luther King Jr. on April 4 and the assassination of Robert F. Kennedy on June 5.

The conventions of both parties of 2020 will also be held during a year of violence, political turbulence, and civil unrest complicated further by the fake-plandemic, a democrat political scheme, following a real pandemic, a Chinese Communist Party biological warfare attack. It has now become clear that democrats are using the pandemic to crater the Trump economy in states and cities they control as well as allowing- nay- promoting violence and insurrection This is as their communist mentors from the past advised them to do many decades ago:

Goal #19. "Use student riots to foment public protests…"

Goal #20. "Infiltrate the press…"

Goal #21. "Gain control of key positions in radio, TV, and pictures."

Goal #22. "Continue discrediting American culture…"

Goal #25. "Break down cultural standards of morality…"

Goal #29. "Discredit the American Constitution…"

Goal #30. "Discredit the American founding fathers…"

Goal #31. "Belittle all forms of American culture and discourage teaching of American History."

Goal #32. "Support any socialist movement to give centralize control of any part of the culture…"

Goal #38. "Transfer some of the powers of arrest from the police to social agencies…"

Goal #40. "Discredit the family as an institution. Encourage promiscuity and easy divorce."

Goal #42. "Create the impression that violence and insurrection are legitimate aspects of the American tradition; that students and special interest groups should rise up and use "united force" to solve economic, political or social problems."

The Democrat Socialist Party owns these communist goals and their consequences in America in 2020.

Having already taken out President Kennedy in 1963, and installed Lyndon Johnson as gangster-in-chief (in my opinion), American and Soviet/Cuban communist thugs were behind much of this unrest and used it all to recruit new revolutionaries as well as "useful idiots" to their cause.

Many of the liberals in Congress, academia, Hollywood, and government today came from this generation of hippies, commies, protestors, rioters, dopers, and do-gooders. Bernie Sanders moved out of his proletariat cabin with a dirt floor, ran for mayor of Burlington, VT, then became a U.S. Senator, and is now running for president of the United States, having lived off the government and his girlfriends/wives all his life … only in America! Joe Biden became a lawyer in 1969 and was elected to the New Castle County Council in 1970. He was elected to the U.S. Senate from Delaware in 1972 when he became the sixth-youngest senator in American history. Biden was reelected six times and was the fourth-most senior senator when he resigned to assume the vice presidency in 2009. Biden has never held a job outside of government but somehow, he and his entire family and many friends have become rich because of his positions of power and influence. Delaware is smaller than many counties in other states. More than half a million businesses, including half of all American publicly traded companies, nearly two-thirds of Fortune 500 companies, and most technology startups have incorporated in Delaware to avoid taxes and other benefits. Do you think quid pro Joe may be receiving some benefits from this unique arrangement? Bill Ayers, Obama's buddy, who almost went to jail for pipe bombing a police station, cut his hair, went to college, and became a professor of English at the University of Chicago. Imagine the damage that guy has done to generations of young impressionable students. David Horowitz, who edited the leftist magazine *Rampart* and helped the Black Panthers organize, converted to conservatism when the Panthers raped, tortured, and murdered his friend and employee.

After Lyndon Johnson declined the democrat presidential nomination at the height of his disastrous Vietnam War and disastrous Great Society programs and War on Poverty, Hubert Humphrey was nominated. Richard Nixon won the election in a landslide of electoral votes but a close popular vote. Nixon got 43.4 percent, Humphrey 42.7 percent, and George Wallace 13.5 percent. Wallace, previously governor of Alabama, carried five states and almost split the conservative vote to elect a democrat, like Ross Perot did in 1992 for Bill Clinton; such were the times. Analysts have argued the election of 1968 permanently disrupted the New Deal Coalition that had dominated presidential politics for thirty-six years. The left was down but not out!

Saul Alinsky, a communist activist and agitator from the 50s, transformed himself into a "community organizer" and completed his life's legacy in 1971. He wrote *Rules for Radicals: A Pragmatic Primer for Realistic Radicals* and it became the new-left's playbook. Alinsky advocated infiltration and subversion of institutions from the inside rather than confrontation and violence. It is the model a young Hillary Clinton and Barack Obama later used in their rise to power. They took Alinsky's ideas to a level he could never have imagined. He died in 1972.

Following the Nixon/Ford debacle, and the one-term Carter malaise, Ronald Reagan—a Trump-like character but with humility, humor, and decorum—became president in January 1981, the year mortgage interest rates hit a record high of 18.3 percent ... one of Carter's many destructive legacies! Reagan, like Trump, turned the economy around, rebuilt the military, reduced regulations, cut taxes, and Iran released our embassy hostages after four-hundred-and-forty-four days of Carter's failure to act decisively. Because of Reagan's policies, the Soviet Union was brought to its knees economically and collapsed during the following administration of George H.W. Bush. Trump is doing the same thing to North Korea and Iran, bankrupting the regimes ... and had China on the ropes until they unleased hell on us and the world in the form of a virus never seen before, perhaps created by a bioweapons lab in Wuhan. This may not prove to be the case, but I would not put it past them ... they are atheist totalitarian communists, with no God to answer to ... but then so are Marxist socialists in America. All Marxist socialists in America are now democrats!

While Ronald Reagan was in the Whitehouse fighting communism, a young Barack Obama, who "sought out Marxist professors and radical students" was soaking it up at Columbia and Harvard, both long time hot beds of pro-Soviet anti-American activity. The Soviet Union collapsed but Russia remained a communist nuclear power and a socialist dictatorship. By this time, American liberals of several generations were infected with the virus of communism and were spreading the disease rapidly. J. Edgar Hoover, the House Un-American Activities Committee (HUAC), and Senator Joe McCarthy attempted to identify, contact trace, and quarantine communists and their sympathizers, but America was heading for a political pandemic of unimaginable proportions. Today a strong majority of America's millennials say they would prefer liberal socialism over conservative capitalism. How did that happen you say…deliberately and with enthusiasm by the communist infiltrated left, accomplishing Goal #17 - "Get control of the schools. Use them as transmission belts for socialism and current Communist propaganda. Soften the curriculum. Get control of teachers' associations. Put the party line in textbooks." They not only got control of the schools and teacher's unions, they got control of the minds and hearts of our children and grandchildren, and we paid them to do it! The left's pursuit of the forty-five goals of communism has caused systemic and transformational changes to America, none of them good! The left—committed communists, socialists, progressives, liberals, and their naïve useful idiots—are now all democrats.

Bill Clinton, who had received a Rhodes Scholarship from Oxford, was elected president in 1992. Barack Obama, having graduated from Columbia University in 1983, and then Harvard Law, taught constitutional law at the University of Chicago Law School from 1992 to 2004. In 1994 the Contract with America, a legislative agenda advocated by the Republican Party, written by Newt Gingrich and Dick Armey, detailed the actions republicans promised to pursue if elected. The voters liked it and republicans became the majority party in the House of Representatives for the first time in forty years. This was a mid-term election during Bill Clinton's first term. The democrat "Imperial Congress" was gone and Newt Gingrich became Speaker of the House. With help from the dot-com boom, Gingrich and Clinton balanced the federal budget and generated a surplus. Congress was quick to begin to spend it like drunken sailors, "the peace dividend" they called it … found money. Subsequent Congresses and presidents ballooned the national debt to over 10 trillion dollars and then Obama and his comrades doubled it again to over 20 trillion dollars. To put this in perspective, this is more debt than from all the presidents from George Washington through George Bush combined!

Bill was a pragmatic liberal and lifetime philanderer, but even many conservatives would agree, a surprisingly good president, thanks to Newt! Hillary was another matter … we did not find out who she really is until she became Senator of NY, then Secretary of State for Obama! The Clintons left the Whitehouse broke, according to Hillary, but over the next several decades leveraged their positions in government into one of the world's largest money laundering schemes, The Clinton Foundation. They are now worth over 100 million dollars. Read Peter Schweitzer's book *Clinton Cash* for details on how they did it. Then there was Benghazi, "extremely careless" handling of classified information, the email evidence deletions, FISA abuse, rigging the democratic primary against Bernie, deep state and Democratic National Committee (DNC) collusion, framing General Flynn, and coup attempt against the duly elected new president, and much much more. Guilty as sin, free as a bird … it's the democrat way!

Obama would take socialism to a whole new level in America. Obamacare, aka the Un-affordable Care Act, took over one-sixth of the U.S. economy in his first two years in office … quite a progressive step forward for the new, mostly unknown, untested, President and his comrades in Congress. With full support and cover from the national media, he doubled the national debt to over 20 trillion dollars with free stuff social spending to dependent constituents but let the military be depleted. He obligated the U.S. to trillions of dollars of donations to major polluters, like China and India, to fight climate change and proposed energy policies and rules that would have crippled the U.S. energy dependent economy. He financed a new round of terrorism for Iran with billions of dollars in cash and let the Syrian civil war get out of hand. Russia and Iran entered that space permanently, ISIS created an unchallenged caliphate in the region, Syria's Assad gassed his own people crossing Obama's red line, North Korea resumed testing nuclear weapons, China continued to eat our lunch with trade deficits and stealing our intellectual property, and Israel was thrown under the bus at every turn … to name a few. Obama has to be objectively the most destructive president in modern American history, eclipsing his close second, Jimmy Carter, and LBJ from decades past.

Obama opened our borders, allowed sanctuary cities, and condoned illegals getting welfare and services while in the U.S. One might look at his record as a failure on many levels, but to him and his comrades it was a resounding success. Communists believe that to replace a decadent capitalist society, you must first burn down or overwhelm what is in place, then rebuild utopia upon the ashes. That is exactly what we see happening in June 2020 with Black Lives Matter, Antifa, and assorted anarchist groups, black and white brainwashed youth, burning, looting, occupying Democrat controlled

America cites. Meanwhile, patriotic law-abiding religious citizens of the silent moral majority, of all races and creeds, are looking forward to November so we can vote these leftist democrats out of office and retake our country. All progressive, socialist, communist, liberal anarchist are democrats. Remember that when you go the polls to vote.

Crooked Hillary was to be heir apparent, successor to Obama. She was to consolidate and expand his gains made in purging and replacing leaders in the Pentagon, Justice Department, FBI, CIA, NSA, IRS, EPA, NASA, NOAA, and the new Consumer Financial Protection Bureau (CFPB) ... an unaccountable agency reporting to the Federal Reserve but having enormous power to not just regulate business with rules and enforcement actions but to force transformation of businesses, or face direct government oversight and scrutiny that would be fatal. Senator Elizabeth Warren championed creation of the CFPB. Jason Chaffetz details this in his book, *Power Grab: The Liberal Scheme to Undermine Trump, the GOP, and Our Republic.* Trump neutralized the CFPB by appointing his Office of Management and Budget head, Mick Mulvaney to replace Obama appointee Richard Cordray as chief of the CFPB.

The cabal of elites in Washington, George Soros, and their fellow travelers were licking their chops at the prospect of a complete and lasting takeover of New Amerika, a socialist utopia in the making. Electing crooked Hillary Clinton would have meant the end of America as we have known it for at least a generation.

The deep state was positioned, sleeper cells were activated, and the election was rigged ... but then along came the man they didn't count on, Donald J. Trump, and just like that—America was back ... no more mandates for Obamacare, Military restored, Paris Climate Accord rejected, Iran Nuke Deal withdrawn, ISIS caliphate destroyed, China challenged on trade and IP, North American Free Trade Agreement (NAFTA) replaced with United States–Mexico–Canada Agreement (USMCA), Trans-Pacific Partnership (TPP) dumped, North Korea nuke testing stopped, Israel relationship restored, taxes cut, job killing regulations eliminated, EPA reigned in, NASA mission renewed, pipelines approved, drilling and fracking encouraged, two conservative Supreme Court Justices and over two hundred federal district judges appointed for life, swamp draining begun, Mexico wall going up, religious liberty defended, FBI director and others fired, and much much more. These are all good things for conservative America but not for liberal/socialist Amerika … not if you are a liberal democrat seeking to transform America into a god-free, gun-free, borderless, classless, egalitarian, socialist, utopian partocracy run by them.

CHAPTER 8
SOCIALISM OR AMERICANISM

Leftists are always thinking about how they can bring down society's institutions and replace them with their own utopian vision of social justice ... repeal and replace! The Biden/Bernie/Bloomberg/Warren strategy is to raise taxes, increase regulations, chase climate change, neuter the military, appease our enemies, coddle our allies, abort our unborn children, indoctrinate our young, confiscate our guns, emasculate our men, deny our God, unionize our schools, occupy Wall Street, corrupt our companies, choke off our energy supplies, subsidize their cronies, etc. ... you get the picture. Create a socialist partocracy, ruled by them. Leftists are all democrats, or worse!

America Rises out of the Ashes!
From a thousand years of oppression and tyranny by the Holy Roman Empire and its acolytes the nobility ... Popes, Kings, Czars, Princes, and Potentates, a few European pilgrims seeking religious freedom braved a treacherous ocean voyage and forged a new country on a new continent with new ideas. Those ideas matured in a hostile environment of toil, struggle, war, determination, and self-reflection for several hundred years before the colonists declared their independence from England in 1776 and established our Constitutional Republic, twelve years later.

After decades of reflection, the new Americans declared to the English monarchy, a type of socialism, "We hold these truths to be self-evident, that all men are created equal, that they are endowed by their Creator with certain unalienable rights, that among these are Life, Liberty and the Pursuit of Happiness" ... the "pursuit" of happiness, not happiness, not even the "right" to happiness. It was a relentless pursuit of happiness with their individual lives, in new-found liberty, with faith in their Creator that made America great in the first place. Now it's happening again. With liberty restored and the chains of bondage broken, we are making America great again! Deniers of the Creator and American exceptionalism are all democrats, or worse!

Ross Perot once said of our European ancestors, "The timid never left, the weak died along the way, and the strong survived to seed a new continent with a hardy stock that would go on to establish the greatest nation the world has ever seen." It is worthy of note the very first pilgrims tried socialism, and it failed miserably, almost costing them their lives due to starvation. But then they allowed the import of African slaves to work the huge agricultural fields in the south, and eventually that too failed miserably, costing over 600,000 lives in the Civil War. Slavery is the only other economic system to fail on all counts as much as socialism. Socialism violates basic human nature and always eventually produces mutually shared poverty, and worse, every time! Democrats were the party of slavery, now they are the party of socialism. All socialists in America today are democrats or worse.

The American Constitution, designed by learned men who knew well the lessons of history, was and still is primarily a constraint on government, not on citizens. Socialism seeks to impose the will of government on the governed whether they like it or not, for their own good, of course ... e.g., Obamacare, Paris Climate Accord, Iran Nuclear Deal, TPP, Medicare-for-All, Green New Deal, New Way Forward bill, Clean Power Plan (aka War on Coal), Waters of the United States (fed jurisdiction over every mud puddle, stream, field, and ditch with water in it), overreach of the EPA, IRS, FBI, CIA, OHSA, RCRA, CERCLA (superfund act—90 percent of $$ to lawyers), solar and wind subsidies, electric car subsidies, ethanol subsidies ... and before that ... LBJ's War on Poverty and Great Society programs, NAFTA, and Federal Aid (and strings) to Education, etc. These programs all come from democrats, or worse!

First Amendment restricting Congress:

"Congress shall make no law respecting an establishment of religion, or prohibiting the free exercise thereof; or abridging the freedom of speech, or of the press; or the right of the people peaceably to assemble, and to petition the government for a redress of grievances"

Religion, especially Christianity, has been under attack in America for decades. Socialists, communists in sheep's clothing, have been relentless to remove prayer from schools and public places, mentions of God, and crosses from public property ... and even the military. But, without faith in a God, our rights become allowed by government, easily alienated ... not endowed by a Creator and unalienable. Democratic socialists, like their true mentor Karl Marx, see God and religion as the "opium of the people," not vital underpinnings of the republic as the founders did.

Free speech, especially on college campuses, is also under attack. Conservatives are shouted down and often physically attacked by liberal students who are seldom held accountable. Liberal professors and administrators created this condition over the past decades. Now it seems the inmates are running the asylum! These violators are all democrats, or worse!

Freedom of the press applies to real free press, not the lying, corrupt, dishonest, fake news, anti-conservative, Trump-hating media mob masquerading as "free" press today. They are free alright, free of integrity! Americans have a right to freedom of speech and a free and honest press that is fair and reports unbiased truth. All biased fake-news media moguls and reporters are democrats or worse!

One of the goals of Soviet communism for the destruction of America from the inside is to "infiltrate and gain control of the Press … radio, TV, and pictures" (Goals 20–21). They have obviously been hugely successful with few exceptions. *Washington Post, New York Times*, CNN, MSNBC, ABC, CBS, NBC … Hannity refers to them as the media mob, an apt description. Thank God, and Rupert Murdock, for Fox News and Fox Business. I think someday we will see a Trump News Channel, and it would be yuuuge! Maybe he will just buy the last remaining conservative network, One America News (OAN). Once Rupert Murdock dies or retires, his two liberal sons will undoubtedly destroy Fox News and Fox Business Channels, transforming it into another liberal mouthpiece for democrats and the left. If all a person watches and reads today is the media mob, they would think America was hell and its president was the anti-Christ. I know some of those people and I will bet you do too! Give them a copy of this book and dare them to read it.

Second Amendment … restricting government—federal, state, local:

> *"A well-regulated Militia, being necessary to the security of a free State, the right of the people to keep and bear Arms, shall not be infringed."*

The framers of the Bill of Rights adapted the wording of this amendment from nearly identical clauses in some of the original thirteen state constitutions. Recognizing the need for the new country to create and maintain a standing army, i.e., "Militia," to maintain "the security of a free State," the framers specifically granted "the people," in addition to the military, the right to keep and bear arms. This was so the people could be safe in their person and homes and not intimidated by the militia. In modern English, the words would be something like,

"Since an armed Military is necessary to the security of a free state, the right of Citizens to also own and carry guns shall not be unduly restricted."

This interpretation has been confirmed by the Supreme Court several times and should form the rationale for declaring an "assault rifle" ban unconstitutional.

That we have senseless and/or politically motivated mass shootings in America today, such as at Marjory Stoneman Douglas high school in Parkland, Florida, last year is the fault of political correctness, not of "we the people" owning and carrying firearms … so says Andrew Pollack, father of Meadow, one of the students killed.

> *"Why Meadow Died*, Pollack's book, is the untold story of how the moral corruption wrought by politically correct policies and willful blindness made the most avoidable school shooting in history somehow inevitable."
> —Bill Bennet, Former U.S. Secretary of Education for Ronald Reagan.

Mass shooters, rioters, anarchist, and other radicals may be the product of Goal #42 which is

> *"Create the impression that violence and insurrection are legitimate aspects of the American tradition; that students and special-interest groups should rise up and use 'united force' to solve economic, political or social problems."*

On reading this, BLM and Antifa, the new left's KKK, come to mind.

John Wilkes Booth who assassinated Lincoln was a disgruntled democrat and Lee Harvey Oswald who assassinated Kennedy was a disgruntled communist sympathizer. Some other violent lefty groups also come to mind … Black Panthers, Weather Underground (Obama's buddy, Bill Ayers group), Students for a Democratic Society (SDS, Tom Hayden's group), Black Lies Matter (sprung up from Obama's mishandling of the Ferguson incident), Antifa, KKK … all democrats or worse. To be fair there are radicals willing to resort to violence on both sides but while the far-right groups mainly just want to be left alone or are retaliating, the far-left groups with social causes seek to change a specific policy or behavior through acting out violently. Social terrorists attempt to force their beliefs on the general population. By this definition, socialists are social terrorists! All socialists are democrats or worse.

Socialist democrats today are relentless in their efforts to effectively repeal our second amendment rights by any means possible while at the same time pushing their political correctness agenda that makes us all less safe. If they gain control of the Whitehouse and Congress … well, just look to the state of Virginia to see what would happen. A bill to ban certain weapons and make pretty much all gun-owners criminals just barely failed in committee, but the gun grabbers will not give up, they will be back.

Bloomberg is the most honest about his goals to eliminate private civilian ownership of guns, but Sanders and Biden feel the same way … Biden telling the steelworker he would ban his "AR-14." John Kerry said he would ban "AR-16s"! Both men are useful, and dangerous, idiots. Confiscation and banning of private ownership of guns, i.e., disarming the public, always precedes socialist dictatorship, e.g., Russia, China, Cuba, Venezuela, Iran, North Korea.

If you value your first and second Amendment rights, do not vote for those who would take them away, i.e., any democrat.

Our American Constitution has been perverted, reviled, twisted, interpreted, distorted, undermined, revised, and denied over the past two-hundred-and-thirty-four years but has proven to be quite durable. It is the only thing that keeps us from becoming a government of men rather than a government of laws. "Men" are fickle, self-serving, scheming, lying, narcissistic … as we have seen over the last few years. The Constitution and the law stand in the breach between order and anarchy.

To the left, the revolution is always the thing, by whatever means necessary! Whatever the issue they are pursuing, whether it is abortion, gun control, health care for all, wealth redistribution, electoral college, etc., it's never the real issue. The real issue is always advancing the revolution to "fundamentally transform America" (Obama's words). These issues are just steppingstones, sometimes meant to disrupt or overwhelm the system, sometimes to advance the cause incrementally.

Architects say to make major changes it is easier to demolish a building first then rebuild with a new design. Leftists have long understood that it is easier to first destroy what is, than to renovate a failed institution into what they believe it should be. Socialism believes capitalism is fatally flawed and systemically incapable of producing social justice for all. Lenin said something like, "We will burn down society and upon the ashes build utopia." This follows the Marxist/Leninist strategy to repeal first, then replace the institutions. They won't admit it, but this is exactly what democrats are trying to do with health care, energy, transportation, immigration, education, family values, sexual morality, science, academia, entertainment, news media, DOJ/FBI, marriage, corporate governance, and every traditional American "institution" that stands in the way of their vision of a socialist utopia of social justice ... which by the way has no successful role model in history.

It is worth repeating Tucker Carlson's commentary on the New Way Forward Act (H.R. 5383), sponsored by forty-four democrats, including all four of AOC's Squad ...

> "It would be the coup de grâce to our already balkanized country, reflecting a radical new Democratic Party that views our nation as a rogue state, in which everything must be destroyed and remade: our laws, our institutions, our freedoms, our history and our values."

This book will provide deep insight into why that statement is "Mostly True," according to Snopes. Sound familiar? Destroy and remake, repeal and replace!

Modern advocates of socialism, especially the young, seem to always think, "Well, that may be but socialism, even communism, is a better system than capitalism. We believe Marx had the right idea, the dictators of Germany, SE Asia, Africa, Russia, China, Cuba, and Venezuela just had a poor implementation of his ideas for social justice, and we can do better this time around." Really???? Where did they get these ideas? At school, college, universities, social/mainstream media all of which were cleverly and intentionally infiltrated by communists plying their ideology over the past sixty years. These "schools" laud the humanity of Marx, Engels, Lenin, and Trotsky as great social justice warriors and denigrate the character of Washington, Jefferson, Adams, and Hamilton as despicable white slave owners.

CHAPTER 9
A MIND, LIKE A CRISIS, IS A TERRIBLE THING TO WASTE

A key institution that communists always seek to dominate is the broad one of education. Soviet and Chinese communists are famous for their forced "reeducation" camps. In America a more subtle approach is needed, and they have become expert at it ... achieving a change in how people think, feel, or act without their ever realizing they have been reeducated ... this is one definition of brainwashing!

> *"Education is the process of facilitating learning, or the acquisition of knowledge, skills, values, beliefs, and habits. Educational methods include teaching, training, storytelling, discussion and directed research. Education can take place in formal or informal settings and any experience that has a formative effect on the way one thinks, feels, or acts may be considered educational."* —Wikipedia

So, education includes schooling, reading, instruction, news, entertainment, protesting, radio, TV, movies, etc. These are all conduits which communists use to ply the minds of unsuspecting individuals, especially the young. When done for nefarious purposes, it is called propaganda.

Below are the goals specific to "education" Do they sound familiar?

17. *"Get control of the schools. Use them as transmission belts for socialism and current communist propaganda. Soften the curriculum. Get control of teachers' associations. Put the party line in textbooks."*

18. *"Gain control of all student newspapers."*

19. *"Use student riots to foment public protests against programs or organizations which are under communist attack."*

20. *"Infiltrate the press. Get control of book-review assignments, editorial writing, and policy-making positions."*

21. *"Gain control of key positions in radio, TV and pictures."*

Historically, over 100 million people were murdered, starved, raped, brutalized, and enslaved trying to enforce communism in the twentieth century. "Well, that was Communism, not Socialism"—they say. This shows extreme ignorance since communist Russia was officially the Union of Soviet *Socialist* Republics (USSR), and Nazi stands for the National *Socialist* German Workers Party. There *is* one significant difference between then and now. Communism typically required its subjects to submit or be murdered at the barrel of a gun, American democratic socialism requires its subjects to commit economic and political suicide at the ballot box, after a period of seduction with free-stuff and plying with identity politics.

The fact that there are more privately owned guns than citizens in America may have a lot to do with that! An armed citizenry will never submit to a socialist dictator, but they may be convinced to vote for one. Germany did in 1933. Hitler did not have a clear majority of the vote but manipulated and intimidated his rise to complete control within a year. Brokered convention anyone?

Gun registration records, kept by a previous regime, fell into the hands of the Nazi government, which used them to disarm its political enemies and the Jews. This is why gun-owner groups like the *National Rifle Association* (NRA) and others fight gun registration. In Florida it is illegal, by statute to keep a database of guns and who owns them, but the FBI seems to be able to track a gun by its serial number, so I doubt confidentiality really exists. Does anyone doubt a Sanders, Biden, Warren, or Bloomberg administration would allow the deep state to use those records against us?

The Democratic Socialist Party in 2020 is asking us to trust them to know best for us and just submit to their benevolent will. Some, like Sanders and Warren, openly admit to their agenda. Others are more subtle and subversive, but they all have the same ultimate agenda for America—to fundamentally transform it from what it is to what they believe it should be, a utopian socialist partocracy run by them ... for our own good, of course.

George Soros is a huge fan and contributor to dozens of groups subverting free-enterprise capitalism and American exceptionalism, i.e., the Democratic Socialist Party and their many comrades in nongovernmental organizations (NGOs), 501(c)(4)s, the fake news media, academia, Hollywood, industry, trial lawyers/American Civil Liberties Union (ACLU), etc. He directs many of his billions made with capitalism to destroy capitalism, which stands in the way of his Open Society utopian dream. All Soros affiliates and collaborators are democrats, or worse. Think about that when you vote!

CHAPTER 10
OBAMA AND TRUMP – POLAR OPPOSITES!

As shown by Obama's plan for recovering from the great recession, democrat socialists trust big government, not Americans, to solve big problems ... with solutions like printing money, near-zero fed interest rate, quantitative easing, bailouts for large corporations and banks, International deals crippling America, increasing welfare payments and food stamps, and taking over one-sixth of the U.S. economy—health care, etc. Admittedly, Obama's policies may have temporarily saved America from going off the cliff, but his recovery had stalled.

If this sounds like the Trump's response to the coronavirus pandemic, it's not—apples and oranges. In 2008, we had a financial crisis of our own making and a very weakened economy. In 2020 we have a health crisis of China's making, but our underlying economy is still strong, just taking a time out to recover from the pandemic.

Even though Obama/Biden doubled the national debt from 10 trillion dollars to 20 trillion dollars over eight years piling up more additional debt than all previous presidents combined, too many jobs had been lost, too many were on welfare of various kinds, including corporate welfare, unemployment was too high, labor participation was too low, trade deficits were excessive, too much government spending was bankrupting our government ... and on top of all that he refinanced Iran's reign of terror in the Middle East with his Iran Deal, and would have crippled the American economy with his signing the Paris Climate Accord.

Being the Marxist-inspired, Muslim-loving, racist bigot that he is, his goal seemed to be to cripple America so that it could never be great again and he was on his way to accomplishing just that. Obama was a socialist on steroids! The nexus of everything anti-traditional-American … a Manchurian Candidate, smooth as silk, deadly as sin … and still is.

Obama said it would "take a magic wand" to bring back manufacturing jobs, "who's going to do that? How are they going to do that?" I believe he did not even want a strong, prosperous, independent, upwardly mobile American workforce. Such people cannot be easily controlled or manipulated.

Well, the magician, Trump, showed up just in time, and just like that—America was back! But it really did not take a magic wand at all, only common sense and belief in the American spirit of exceptionalism which had been stifled for many years by our own federal government and "stupid politicians," Trump calls them. Trump's plan for making America great again did not depend on his economic brilliance, Ivy League academics, government largess, or socialist redistribution of wealth. Trump's plan for making America great also did not depend on him being "presidential," it depended on letting Americans be Americans, getting government out of the way, out of our pocketbooks, and out of our lives.

Trump trusted the American entrepreneurs, blue-collar workers, farmers, professionals, and businessmen to revive the economy … and a rebuilt military with new rules of engagement. He just got the government out of the way by massively cutting taxes and job killing regulations, and renegotiating international trade deals with Mexico, Canada, China, Japan, South Korea and reinstituting Reagan's "Peace through Strength" initiative. Americans did the rest, and in under three years, 90 percent are now happy with their personal lives, as per Gallop Poll, and 71 percent are happy with Trump's handling of the economy, and his overall job approval rating is 50 percent and climbing ... all economic indicators and metrics at an all-time high, setting records every week. Well, until the Chinese Communist Party sabotaged America and the world with their coronavirus.

We will survive that better than most countries because America is stronger than it's ever been in every way ... because of President Trump's policies. Democrats are hoping he fumbles the ball, and they and their comrades in the fake news media will be trying to make it happen even if it costs lots of American jobs and lives. Yes, after watching the shameful and treasonous way they have behaved since the 2016 election, I really do believe that. In England, the minority party calls themselves The Loyal Opposition, in America the minority party calls themselves The Resistance, a term of war! All traitors in the Resistance are democrats or worse.

If you are a liberal, progressive, leftist, socialist democrat (lots of redundancy there), there is plenty not to like about Trump! He has almost single-handedly reversed decades of "progress" for them and put their ultimate agenda in jeopardy. They know another term of Trump will set them back a generation. More lifetime federal judges (over two-hundred-and-twenty now) and Supreme Court appointments (two now, one hanging by a thread) alone will establish a firewall against their return to power for decades. Republicans must retain the Whitehouse and the Senate for that to continue! Even liberal Wall Streeters are telling Charlie Gasparini, Fox's financial gadfly, that if Biden is elected and democrats take the House and Senate, it would be the end of the world for them. They said that before coronavirus panic set in, but this is just a preview of what would happen the day after democrats take back the government, heaven forbid! We will recover from the coronavirus panic and bounce back strongly and quickly but electing democrats to run the country would be catastrophic, I believe.

Conservatives hope this setback for the left lasts until the millennials get good jobs, pay lots of taxes, buy a home, start families, and join their parents and grandparents in being the next greatest generation, not the next snowflake generation. A hopeful sign is that Fox Business reports the housing buyers' market is 48 percent millennials … with cash down payments … maybe living in their parents' basement for a while has paid off.

CHAPTER 11
SCHOOL CHOICE

The government, liberals, and unions seek a monopoly on public education. To give us time to turn around the next generation of grade and high school students, we should be providing school choice, a Trump position, allowing parents to remove their children from failing government schools, run by liberal school boards, socialist democrats, and teachers unions, and place them in nongovernment, union free, charter, private, and faith-based schools, and supporting homeschool cooperatives and other alternative education not under direct federal government influence or control.

Here's a plan to consider: Money allocated by state and federal government for K-12 should follow the child, whose parents/guardians would pay the school of their choice with a voucher. This would only apply to any child maintaining a C average. Any child not maintaining a C average is not being educated anyway, so ... if they don't, it's back to the nearest failing union run public school for babysitting ... not left behind, just left alone, so as not to drag down students who want to learn. Special needs and exceptions could be accommodated humanely, of course.

You can lead a horse to water, but if he will not drink you put him back in the barn, don't hitch him up to the stagecoach and jeopardize the journey for the others. Curriculums should not be "softened" or "dumbed down" to accommodate any race, creed, color, national origin, or sexual orientation. To do so is to admit a sub-group is inferior because of their differentiation by same.

For example, if the cost for educating one child in public school is $12,000 per year, a realistic mean between NY and MS, parents or guardians could designate $1,000/month per child to the educators of their choice, whoever they may be, by voucher or other means ... with minimum standards, but not strings, attached ... like charter schools operate. This would undoubtedly create competition and improved outcomes, as charter schools have. The NEA denies this incontrovertible fact ... of course they do! Parents/guardians would have the right to review curriculum and textbooks and interview teachers for each class and opt out or jump ship if they do not approve. Conservative Christian parents would not be forced to put up with liberal irreligious teachers or administrations, sacrificing their child's one shot at being educated on the altar of political correctness, or tolerating and accommodating bad behavior from other students leading to violence like the mass shooting at Margorie Stoneman Douglass high school.

Since money for public financed education is coming from all American taxpayers not just parents, citizens deserve to get their money's worth here ... and that is an educated, productive, patriotic, physically fit, well-mannered, English speaking, non-smoking, drug-free, job-skilled, law-abiding citizen heading for college, vocational school, military, or a full-time job at the age of eighteen. The investment in one student would be 13 grade years x $12,000 = $156,000! Consider continuing that $1000/month for two years if the K-12 graduate would attend a technical/trade school or junior college close to home, not for a country club college run by liberal administrators and liberal tenured professors. Any taxpayer guaranteed "student loans" for higher education should be conditioned on the job market available to pay them back quickly, i.e., no loans for useless degrees, or those "studies" type courses by liberal professors simply seeking to indoctrinate young students! And if the student does not complete the program the grant reverts to a debt to be paid back like a loan, with interest.

Standing for the Pledge of Allegiance and a prayer to our "Creator" would be said before each school day, like it always was in the 50s and 60s. Those failing to show respect for our flag and America's Creator ... you got it, back to the failing union run public school for babysitting. Make sense, sound reasonable ... not to democrats and socialists.

Liberal socialist democrats would oppose this with everything they have, as they want to continue controlling the content of education, indoctrinating our youth, and receiving payouts from the public teachers' unions, just like their Soviet communist mentors advised them to do seventy-five years ago:

> "Teachers unions have steadily amped up their political involvement: From 2004 to 2016, their donations grew from $4.3 million to more than $32 million—an all-time high. Even more than most labor unions, they have little use for republicans, giving democrats at least 94 percent of the funds, they contributed to candidates and parties since as far back as 1990, where our data begins.

> "Two organizations account for practically all of the contributions made by teachers' unions: The National Education Association (about $20 million in 2016) and the American Federation of Teachers (almost $12 million). Both groups—which compete for members, but also collaborate with each other through the NEA-AFT Partnership—are Soros affiliates and consistently among the organizations that contribute the most money to candidates and political groups." —OpenSecrets.org

All teachers' union leadership are democrats, or worse.

Goal #17: *Gain control of the schools. Use them as transmission belts for socialism and current communist propaganda. Soften (dumb down) the curriculum. Get control of teachers' associations. Put the (communist) party line in textbooks.*

I did not make this stuff up, folks, it came from the communist Soviet Union in the 40s and 50s.

Most public and private universities are already lost to liberal tenured professors and bloated administrations who are running a breeding ground for future anti-American Marxists, not educating our children to be independent thinkers and productive, patriotic, tax-paying, law-abiding, contributing citizens. Taxpayer guaranteed student loans and grants should not be available to universities who deny free speech, conservative or liberal, in class or on campus, allow any violence or intimidation from the left or right, and professors should be censured, fined, or fired for intimidating or downgrading any student who respectfully opposes their liberal or conservative views and teaching, i.e., recognizing the students first amendment rights and the right to due process for violations thereof. President Trump recently signed an executive order along those lines, but aggressive enforcement is needed

So-called "Studies" classes should not be required for any curriculum qualified for loans and grants. These are classes where the liberal professor picks a politically correct premise, like America is a Racist Country, or White Men are Chauvinist Pigs, and then proceeds to prove it to unwitting students whether they like it or not. Of course, they wouldn't name the class that. American Racial Studies and Male Proclivity Studies would be more appealing and deceptive. Victor Davis Hansen, PhD, of Stanford says that twenty-five years ago there were very few "studies" courses at major universities, now as much as 25 percent or more of the total class offerings are "studies" courses, and they are extremely popular with students. At that age who would not prefer studying a politically correct topic with a cool liberal Marxist professor to studying physics, chemistry, math, and engineering with a nerd with a pocket protector. Barack Obama certainly did. He said, "When in college I sought out the Marxist professors and radical students." All Marxist professors and radical students are democrats, or worse!

Nationally, both tuition and admin-to-teacher ratios have increased in direct proportion to the availability of federally guaranteed student loans, and now student debt is larger than total credit card debt in America. How did this happen? It was deliberate, it was calculating, and it is tragic, but another intended consequence of socialism's takeover of education. What would be unthinkable in the baby-boomers' day is now commonplace. Children are signing up for years or decades of indentured servitude when they take out student loans to attend these overpriced country clubs for liberals and, if they finish, many end up with worthless degrees, flipping burgers at McDonalds, or living on Mommy's and Daddy's credit cards.

Current law is that not even bankruptcy forgives student loans. Democrats want to pander to students by offering forgiveness of their loans. What does that say to those who took a job because they couldn't afford or didn't want to go to college, or those who worked two jobs so they could afford to go to college, or those who have a mortgage loan, or a business loan, or a car loan. Forgiveness of loans is immoral and un-American … but then so is Socialism!

If you want to give your child the gift of a loan-free, liberal-free, government-free, conservative education as good as any in the country, consider a conservative college like Hillsdale College or Liberty University. If your child attends a major public or private university, do not be surprised if they come back a cynical liberal socialist like the majority of their peers today.

Good-paying jobs in a free-market economy are about providing a thing of great value, a product or service, to another party who is willing to pay for that value. Pay and price are established by "the market," i.e., what a buying party perceives as worth paying to a producing or supplying party ... the "law of supply and demand." Hence, the starting salary for a physical therapist, an aeronautical engineer, or computer programmer is much higher than a liberal arts major with no marketable skills. Under communism people are required to hold a job according to their ability and get paid according to their need. Sounds fair, right?

Human nature, which never changes no matter what century it is, defeats this socialist idea every time it is tried. Think about it ... no ambitious person in America is going to accept being told what his "need" is, or that his "ability" can be defined by someone else. The law of supply and demand, the foundation of American free-enterprise capitalism is antithetical to communism and socialism. Real Americans prefer maximum freedom to be all they can be, do what they want, and achieve as much as possible. Socialists prefer free stuff and equal outcomes to freedom and merit-based achievement. All socialists are democrats or worse.

CHAPTER 12
THE LEFT'S WAR ON RELIGION

Other aspects of socialism/communism include a disdain for religion, of any kind, but especially Judaism and Christianity. A reformed American communist named David Horowitz recently (2018) wrote a book, one of dozens from him, called *Dark Agenda: The War to Destroy Christian America*. He explains in this, and other books he has written, that a belief in a Creator or God who cares about each individual soul is anathema to the communist worldview and foundational principles. He is a Jew by birth, to a couple of immigrant, nonviolent communist parents in Queens, NY, who longed for the establishment of a Soviet state in America ... go figure! They were not practicing religious Jews and he says he is an agnostic, meaning ... "I just do not know whether there is a god or not."

Horowitz, like Jefferson a man of the Enlightenment (Age of Reason) doesn't believe in miracles, the deity of Jesus, and other supernatural aspects of religion but does believe strongly that faith in God and the practice of religion are vital underpinnings of the American experiment. An older friend told me many years ago, "Christianity would be a good way to live even if it's not true." Being a young Christian at the time I took offense to that, but objectively he was correct. "Endowed by their Creator with certain unalienable rights...," words written by Jefferson have no meaning without a literal Creator God. Hopefully, Jefferson made his peace with the true God before he and John Adams died on the same day at the same time, July 4, 1826, just twenty-two years before Karl Marx would publish his atheist *Communist Manifesto*.

Our rights are endowed by God, not allowed by government, a king, a pope, a dictator, or even Congress. And just as importantly, "unalienable" means they cannot be alienated, or separated, or taken away by anyone other than God himself. Liberal socialists, who do not believe in God anyway, ignore this. They want us to voluntarily give up our individual liberty, freedom, and rights at the ballot box so they can create a collective Amerikan utopia where all the women are beautiful, all the men are handsome, and all children are above average … with participation trophies for all—where all citizens, documented or undocumented, are equal, but some are more equal than others. One nation, under Biden, undivided, with environmental, financial, and social justice for all, except deplorables! No need for "under God" in a Sanders or Biden socialist administration. They would probably eliminate it from the pledge by executive action.

Marx, with backup from his contemporary Charles Darwin, went to great lengths to deny the existence of a supernatural, non-material, god. To Marx, the universe, which he thought had always been, is just a mass of particles (matter) operating undirected in a field of forces like gravity and that somehow it all just evolved over time into what he saw in his day. Life to Marx was just another path taken by evolution, and man's intelligent existence was nothing more than happenchance. He called this "dialectical materialism."

He, like many liberals today, was happy to read Darwin's evolution of species since it confirmed his godless, materialistic, happenchance theory of the universe. Marx's real interest was not in natural evolution of species like Darwin, but in the political evolution of human order. He simply dismissed any notion of a Creator God and any moral or consequential constraints that God may have put on his creation, especially on mankind. To Marx, man was the "consummate beast," master of his own destiny, and king of the realm.

To Darwin, man was at the top of a tree of life's evolution. It started somehow in a primordial prebiotic saltwater chemical soup where small molecules became big molecules and came together in violation of everything we now know about physics and synthetic organic chemistry, then through undirected random mutations and survival of the fittest over very long periods of time, intelligent man emerged. Sounds absurd? I always thought so!

Many renowned scientists today say the probability of this happening is astronomically low even over the lifetime of the known universe, ~13+billion years. Darwin could explain aspects of the *survival* of the fittest like beak length and fur color, but even he admitted he could not explain the *arrival* of the fittest, meaning the first cell or the transition between species during the Cambrian explosion of different body types. Both men denied emphatically that life on earth had any linkage to an intelligent or divine agent who caused it for some reason only religion or superstition could propose.

Educated intelligent conservatives, including many prominent scientists, believe they were both fundamentally wrong, for sound scientific reasons, not just religious ones. Marx and Darwin were both atheists, but they are not anymore.

To Marx, religion was the "opium of the people," dulling their sense of curiosity and reason, preventing them from exploring the true nature of man and society. Since, according to Marx and Darwin, man had no obligation to a god, and was not created to serve an absent master, Marx proposed that man was neither good nor bad, and that it was society and institutions that had caused the tyranny, despair, and injustice he saw all around him in mid-nineteenth century Europe. If he could just fix society and the institutions in it, man could then rationally develop a utopia of social justice, peace, equality, and harmony for all. This is the democrat's fix for their Amerika. Four of the institutions Marx singled out for elimination were capitalism, religion, private property, and marriage. Marx considered the evolution from capitalism to socialism and communism to be inevitable and called it social evolution. Lenin, a Marxist devotee, got tired of waiting and launched his Bolshevik revolution in 1917, the rest as they say is history—bloody history.

On the other hand, Christianity, as well as most deist religions, believes that man is a fallen, naturally sinful, creature who is in need of redemption from his Creator God, and that it is impossible to create "heaven on earth," i.e., utopia. Our founders knew this by experience and belief and that is why they set up America as a nation of laws, not of men. Unlike Marx, our founders were under no illusion that man or his institutions could ever be perfected.

Europe, from whence most immigrants came was nations of men, not of laws. The kings, popes, and potentates made up the rules to suit themselves and their subjects were compelled to comply, or else. Later a few wealthy capitalists owned all the money and means of production and the workers, displaced serfs from a previous era, had nothing … no life, no liberty, no property, no happiness, no free stuff. This was the unjust world Marx and Engels railed against in the mid-nineteenth century … and with just cause. However, their proposed cure, socialism/communism, would prove more deadly than the disease they sought to cure.

America's founders, a hundred years earlier, knew men would continue to sin and fail, so with consent of the governed, they wisely proposed to simply constrain, not perfect, society and government with a Constitution and laws rather than follow the centuries old European model. The Constitution they created sought to prevent the greatest sin and failure they could imagine, the gradual expansion of government to take away the freedom and possessions of the people. This is the sin and universal failure of socialism. Washington, Jefferson, Adams, Hamilton, and the others would be shocked to see how far the country they founded has fallen.

Soviet communists, heirs of Karl Marx's legacy, proposed to eliminate the influence of religion in America. Three of the goals were:

1. *Infiltrate the churches and replace revealed religion with "social" religion. Discredit the Bible and emphasize the need for intellectual maturity which does not need a "religious crutch."*

2. *Eliminate prayer or any phase of religious expression in the schools on the grounds that it violates the principle of "separation of church and state."*

3. *Use technical decisions of the courts to weaken basic American institutions by claiming their activities violate rights.*

Liberals have been pursuing these goals for decades, with great success! All liberals are democrats, or worse.

The first step in converting someone to communism to betray their country is getting them to join their recruiter in rejecting God. Belief in a Creator God is at the core of the American experiment we call the United States of America. Disbelief in any God is at the core of the Marxist experiment, they call it Materialistic Socialism. Hence, Horowitz title, *The War to Destroy Christian America*, is a Marxist/socialist/communist war against our Creator God, Christian America, and everything and everyone pro-life Christian conservatives hold dear. All such antagonist are democrats or worse!

The American experiment as we now know has been wildly successful despite notable national sins and failures like slavery, treatment of native Americans, LBJ's Great Society, Roe v. Wade, Obamacare, open borders and sanctuary cities, drug addiction, human trafficking, homelessness, invasion of Iraq, deep state corruption, Benghazi – lies and dereliction of duty, Russia hoax, Ukraine hoax, Impeachment hoax, etc. Through it all, including numerous wars, America and its Constitution have proved a durable model, the

envy of the world. America is great because its people are good …
and religious! Let's keep America great!

CHAPTER 13
JUST WHAT IS SOCIALISM ANYWAY?

The classic Marxian definition of socialism is the central control of the means of production and distribution. Marx built his entire case around the history of the world being that of class struggles and saw this as a binary problem which naturally evolves over time, i.e., one class against another class. For him it was the proletariats (workers) against the bourgeoise (capitalists). To Marx, economics was at the heart of the problem, the haves versus the have-nots. What he called "surplus value," we now call profits. Marx contended the ones who did the work deserved the profits, not the capitalists who only provided money for which they had already collected interest. His solution was socialism, which he called communism.

He, and his young comrade Engels, described how and why everything should work in a painfully detailed set of volumes called *Das Kapital*, which few ever read. But his short work *The Communist Manifesto* was a blockbuster, printed and distributed in every language of most of the "civilized" world. By the mid-twentieth century, a hundred years in print, it defined the foundational principles which ruled 60 percent of the world ... USSR (Russia and their eastern European satellites), National Socialist German Workers Party (Nazis), Peoples Republic of China, India, North Korea, most of Africa, Cuba, and much of South America. After World War II,

America and England increasingly adopted socialist policies, until Ronald Reagan and Margaret Thatcher came along and pulled them back from the brink circa 1980–88, but then they both backslid … until Donald Trump and Boris Johnson came along! We don't have to ever accept the inevitability of defeat or capitulation to anti-American socialism, as long as we can vote and own guns.

No single person other than Jesus Christ has had as much influence over humankind as Karl Marx … and for Marx, never in a good way! By my count, by 2020, about two dozen countries have tried Marxian socialism in various forms, all with the same result … mutually shared poverty and tyranny for the citizens, riches and power for the ruling class. The only economic system to fail on all counts more than socialism is slavery. No country today has a pro-slavery party. America's democrat party was the last party of slavery, now they are the party of socialism, a close cousin to slavery.

But socialism is not just about the making and distribution of money. Heavy-handed centralized control and regulation of critical institutions like health care, energy, transportation, industry, welfare, taxation, environment, business, and even social institutions like marriage, morality, private property, and religion are also socialism. Sounds like any country you know? No, not Russia, Cuba, China, or Venezuela, it is Obama's Amerika, and is what Biden, Sanders, and all liberal democrats also want. That is why Bernie calls himself a democratic socialist. It is who they all are even if they deny the name. Their party platform in 2020 is all about gaining more control, acquiring more jurisdiction, redistributing more wealth, all in the name of spreading more social justice.

Marx proposed it was these very institutions that created and sustained injustice in the world and that they should all be abolished and just turn it all over to the proletariats. George Soros agrees but they all know that before their vision of a classless, stateless, borderless, gun-free, carbon-free, religion-free, socialist utopia can be created they must first get control, not just of the means of production, but the institutions of production.

CHAPTER 14
MAKE AMERICA LAST AGAIN

Communists, democrats, socialists, Soros, and their comrades in congress, the courts, the media, Hollywood, Wall Street, academia, deep state, and Unions almost succeeded in destroying America from the inside and replacing it with a classless, borderless, stateless, godless, globalist government Soros calls an "open society," and democrats call "democratic socialism.

For eight long years, through illegal actions and collusion with his comrades in arms, Barack Obama did his best to cripple America so that it could never be great again, and Hillary Clinton was anointed to complete the coup d'état the new-left had been patiently pursuing since the early 60s; the players were in position, the deep state was empowered, sleeper cells were activated, the election was fixed … but, then God and Donald J. Trump showed up, and just like that … *America was Back!*

This is not about the 2016 election, the Russia witch hunt, the impeachment hearings, the IG Reports, or the Durham prosecutions, it is about how we got here, and why America is still in imminent peril. The current leftist coup has been exposed and the republic saved, but the rogue agents inside and outside government who avoided jail or banishment will be trying even harder this time to make sure they stop Donald Trump from being elected to another term. They know if he is reelected, it will be Trump *Unleashed* ... on them! *Draining* the swamp will take on a speed and scale that will be better described as *dredging* the Swamp! This war of cultures will rage on, even if Trump is reelected.

Trump is the mortal enemy of the left which has been making steady progress for the last sixty years. Another term of Trump unleashed will set them back a generation. Because they know this, there is no crime they are not willing to commit or lie they are not willing to tell to stop him. Recent impeachment actions are an example but won't be the end. I suspect they had something to do with the coronavirus pandemic and panic in America. Another four more years of Trump unleashed will put a stake through their black evil communist hearts for at least a generation.

What we are seeing in politics today is the culmination of almost hundred years of international political and social revolution, not just some recent isolated periodic shifts in public mood or opinion, i.e., the "swinging pendulum" model.

This is now a full-on open revolution, and the fate of America and perhaps the entire free world depends on who wins. Reagan realized there could be no lasting "peaceful co-existence" with communists, and Trump realizes the same about democratic socialists (communists by another name).

Dinesh D'Souza says, "Trump did not create all this division and descension we see today, it created him." Reluctantly stepping into the spotlight from nowhere respected, like Paul of the Bible, Trump seems to have been anointed with supernatural energy, purpose, and commitment. D'Souza also says, "Trump is a mud wrestler, perhaps just what we needed at this time. Trump is like a pig ... but when you decide to mud wrestle with a pig, realize that the pig loves it, and is probably better adapted to it than most!" After working for twenty hours a day, Trump seems to arise at 4 a.m. every morning thinking how he can befuddle, harass, and distract the morons in the media and the commies in Congress, while at the same time executing end-around, hail Mary, and quarterback draw plays right down the field ... winning, winning, winning for Americans.

Democrats today seem to prefer the vision of Marx, Lenin, Stalin, LBJ, Soros, Alinsky, Clinton, Obama, Biden, Sanders, and Warren over Locke, Montesquieu, Washington, Jefferson, JFK, Reagan and Trump ... go figure! There are only two sides to this coin, and democrats are on the side associated with communism. Voting for a democrat is akin to voting for a communist!

With roots that go back to Karl Marx, the Democratic Socialist revolution winds its way through American history from Roosevelt in the 30s and 40s, through LBJ in the 60s and 70s, to Obama/Clinton in our time. Its ideology, strategies, and tactics are well-documented and easily recognized. We can clearly see the results of past policies and leaders; we can only speculate what crooked Hillary Clinton would have done to America but we can project that she would have consolidated the power of the deep state and Shadow Party, set up by Obama, Soros, and their ilk, around herself in an impenetrable shield that would, by design, be difficult to penetrate in the next twenty years or so.

Revenge on her enemies, elimination of all opposition, expanding the illicit power of the deep state agencies like the FBI, IRS, CIA, EPA, and making structural changes to the Supreme Court makeup, the electoral college rules, EPA authorities, etc. under her unscrupulous control would have been the driving motivations in the first term. Record suicides and random murders would be a hallmark of her administration's legacy. Her second term would thus be assured. America would never be the same after eight years of rule by the most ambitious corrupt embittered leftist shrew the world has ever seen. America dodged a bullet in 2016, but another one is coming our way in 2020.

We conservatives wake every morning just wanting to be left alone to live our lives as we see fit within the constitution and the law, according to our faith in God, as we understand Him. Liberals wake up every morning trying to figure out how they can impose their superior and benevolent will on the rest of us ... for our own good, of course!

Your vote in 2020, and 2022, is literally for the life, or the death, of traditional America.

CHAPTER 15
UNDERSTANDING THE LEFT

The 2016 election of Donald J. Trump marked a new era in American political life. Never has a political apparatchik inside our government attacked the candidate of the other party for president, then the president-elect, then the newly inaugurated president himself with such brazen ferocity and vitriolic hatred … and with impunity, so far at least! And they are still at it near the end of his first term in office. We can document the confluence of politics and philosophies, legends and leaders, liars and leakers over the past hundred years that brought us to this sorry state, with a focus on relevance, i.e., what this means to us in 2020.

Since Trump's election, democrats have put forth no popular ideas and have no accomplishments, only obstruction of Trump, so they see their only path back to power as a scorched earth policy, creating economic and social chaos, strife, dissention, hatred, fear, loathing, and lies. Having failed in their attempt to frame Trump for Russian collusion, obstruction of justice, and quid pro quo in the Ukraine impeachment circus, several have said it would be worth a severe recession to get rid of Trump and tried to make it happen. But the Trump economy is so strong, most have abandoned that strategy in favor of an act of desperation … a party-line, purely political, impeachment of the president of the United States. Their comrades in the media, Hollywood, academia, and many "orderly institution-alists" in banking, wall street, big tech, and industry are all in. They have universal disdain for Trump and the conservatives who support him, referring to these supporters as irredeemable deplorables! Could the coronavirus pandemic panic be their doing? I wouldn't put it past them as they are now truly desperate.

True to their Marxist heritage, the left's first instinct is to burn down or overwhelm the system, then upon the ashes rebuild a uto-pian socialist society that brings about their version of social justice, equality, peace, and tranquility to all the earth's children. More tact-ful and covert socialists might call this bringing "order out of chaos." I don't doubt their well-meaning intentions, but that's what makes them all the more dangerous. They always justify their hurtful, harmful, and sometimes violent actions as noble "class struggles," better known today as "identify politics," where temporary pain jus-tifies long-term gain. It could be called the game of "victims and vil-lains"! Since they self-righteously claim to occupy the high ground, ultimately seeking to bring about a better world for all, to them the end justifies the means.

They see themselves as the knights in shining armor whose destiny and duty it is to vanquish the villains and save the victims. Throughout the history of socialism, tried and failed now in twen-ty-four countries, this always involves redistribution of wealth and power from the haves to the have-nots, but always results in mutu-ally shared poverty and tyranny for all but the elite puppet masters in charge. Their games don't work without both victims and villains … blacks/whites, poor/rich, workers/capitalists, gays/straights, women/men, Hispanics/Americans, illegals/citizens, and under-privileged/privileged. Being a victim implies someone else is guilty and if socialists can successfully lay the guilt trip on their marks, the mark will capitulate, cave, withdraw, give in, and relinquish their moral authority whenever challenged aggressively.

White guilt is a prime, but not the only, example of this tactic. When "white guilt" is accepted by whites, the socialists (e.g., democrats) and their victim clients (e.g., blacks) can just claim the possessions and power rightfully earned by the marks (e.g., whites). This scheme is breaking down today because the democrats overplayed their hand, and now we deplorables don't feel guilty anymore, we are just angry and giving as good as we get … i.e., counter punching!

There is power in political incorrectness when you have moral authority. Moral authority comes from knowing your own heart. Moral courage is standing up to those who would attempt to define you otherwise. Only a person, like Trump, who knows he is not a racist, retains the moral authority to call out a legend of the civil rights movement, Elijah Cummings (RIP), for running a "rat-infested shit hole" district like Baltimore, and then double down when criticized. The left has no power over a person who has a good heart and knows it! I'm in the Trump camp!

What follows is for those who want to save America from those self-proclaimed knights of the realm like Obama, Clinton, Biden, Sanders, Warren, and other fellow travelers and comrades in the media, academia, Hollywood, unions, globalists, coastal elites, and their ilk who want to fundamentally transform America from what it is, a center-right free-market constitutional republic, to what they believe it should be, a far-left socialist bureaucratic partocracy … run by them, of course!

If you think it's daunting, remember the lesson of Ronald Reagan and the USSR (Union of Soviet Socialist Republics) known as communist Russia to many. Reagan was elected at the height of the cold war; the nuclear threat had never been higher. Defeating the Soviet Union was considered impossible by everyone in Washington … except Reagan. When asked what his strategy to defeat them was he said, "It's simple, we are right, they are wrong … we are going to win, they are going to lose!" And he set about making it happen, without ever firing a shot or dropping a bomb.

There was absolutely no moral ambivalence with Reagan toward communism because he knew them and their ways well. The left today is literally advocating communism, just without guns to our heads, yet! They call it democratic socialism. Through seduction, lies, subterfuge, and promises of free stuff, democrats are asking Americans to voluntarily commit economic, moral, political, and social suicide at the ballot box. I hope to convince the reader not to fall for it.

By the way, recent polls show that 69 percent of college students would vote for the democrat socialist ticket in 2020, only 23 percent for Trump. The numbers for young millennials without high-paying jobs are similar. These are our children and grandchildren! Maybe we should have a family discussion about this. After reading this book, you will have lots of talking points to discuss with them.

I'm prepared to say with Reagan ... we are right, they are wrong; we are going to win, they are going to lose! Are you? My goal in writing this book is that if you read it with an open mind, you will come away with a keen awareness of who the real enemies of American democracy are and a patriotic commitment to defeat their plans for the fundamental transformation of America into what they believe it should be.

The progressive left has long sought to "repeal and replace America." They hate the very idea of traditional America, American values, the American dream, and especially American exceptionalism. They seem to prefer the slogan "America last," rather than "America first." The election of Hillary Clinton was to be their coup d'état. They failed but will try harder this time, pulling out all the stops, risking everything. All progressive leftists are democrats or worse.

Democrats have proved there is not a crime they are not willing to commit or lie they are not willing to tell to make sure they don't fail again ... it's life or death for them, and they know it! In contrast, the conservative right seeks to make America great again, keep

America great, and promote America first by continuing the policies of the Trump administration for another four years. It is no exaggeration to say that the 2020 elections shall be the most consequential and conspiratorial since Kennedy was elected in 1960, and we all know how that turned out. The same forces of evil, communism, and gangsterism are at play in 2020, inside and outside the government.

Since the Russia witch hunt and Ukranian impeachment, both failed, I expect the desperate commie democrats to attempt to execute their ultimate "insurance policy" to prevent Trump from taking office again. Be aware that Nancy Pelosi is third in line to assume the presidency if anything happens simultaneously to both the president and vice president. If Trump wins reelection, it will be Armageddon for the deep state resistance operatives in Congress, White House, State Department, Secret Service, Pentagon, DOJ, FBI, CIA, NSA, IRS, EPA, and others. It will almost certainly mean the appointment of another conservative Supreme Court Justice and a 6–3 conservative majority, the left's worst nightmare.

Watch your back, Trump!

CHAPTER 16
THE MODUS OPERANDI (MO) OF THE LEFT

This is not conspiracy *theory*, it's what they do, it's how they think, it's how they operate. LBJ's Great Society, De Blasio's NYC, Obamacare, the Southern border crisis, the green new deal, Medicare-for-All are recent examples. What *is* a conspiracy, not just a theory, is the cabal of wealthy individuals, NGOs, corporate moguls, and new-left activists who are loosely organized and funded by George Soros, Tom Steyer, Emilie's List, Progressive Insurance, Jane Fonda, and others to be named in this book.

This cabal sponsored by George Soros is what David Horowitz calls the Shadow Party. Soros is the most extreme of international socialists, if we could even call him that. His desire for the world is beyond the pale. He is the quintessential Marxist man, advocate for "full communism," not just the dictatorship of the proletariat, or economic socialism, but a classless, stateless one world order he calls an Open Society. If he were not so old, I'd wonder if he might be the anti-Christ! Socialism, Soros, Shadow Party ... all left-wing liberal, communistic ... and today's democrat socialist Part represents them all at the ballot box. You may say, I'm a democrat and I'm not a communist, or even a socialist ... I'm a good person, go to church, belong to Kiwanis, etc. Well, according to Lenin and Alinsky, that would make you a "useful idiot" to their cause. A vote for any democrat today is a vote for socialism or worse. This is not the party of JFK anymore.

So, how has socialism worked out for any country who's ever tried it? Where is that utopian model that we are told works so well? History tells us socialism on a large scale always results in mutually shared poverty, misery, tyranny, and death. That's OK with Soros, just gets rid of the clutter of resistance. Russia, China, North Korea, Southeast Asia, Africa, Venezuela, and Cuba murdered over 100 million people imposing socialism over the last hundred years.

Closer to home, Burgess Owens, of NFL fame, testified to Congress of the tragic plight of the black community under LBJ's War on Poverty, Civil Rights Act, and Great Society—all socialist programs that put blacks in dependence on government handouts which led to poverty, crime, illiteracy, illegitimacy, fatherless children, single mother homes. Owens says democrats owe the black community reparations for what this cynical, near genocide, of black culture and family in America by democrats.

Dinesh DeSousa says that LBJ was a former member of the KKK and an overt racist who didn't really give a damn about the Negro, only wanted their votes. LBJ's heart can be felt in his statement to southern democrats to get their support, "I'll have them niggars vot'n democrat for the next 200 years," and today 90 percent still do! White democrat, pro-abortion, socialist liberals became the new massas for a new generation of black voters.

But socialism could never happen in America you say. I recently talked with a man who came to the U.S. from Venezuela thirty-five years ago. He said first came socialism, then disarming the population, then communism, then the tyranny of Chavez, nationalization of the oil industry (CITGO), take over by a dictator Maduro, and now look at it … completely in ruins, occupied by Russia and Cuba proxies. He was warning me to not let it take hold here.

Lefty democrats are not ignorant. In fact, they are probably more educated than Trump's deplorables on average. So why can't they see that what they want and are doing is destructive? Reagan hit the nail on the head when he said, "It's not that our liberal friends are ignorant, it's that they know so much that isn't so." And there is another factor, they see themselves as not only morally and intellectually superior but to have a duty to assume power and control over every aspect of the lives of the underclass, for their own good, of course, while exempting themselves from the same rules. Today's liberal democrats, institutional republicans, the mainstream media, Hollywood, academia, and many industry leaders feel the same way.

They tell we deplorables, "you have many problems and issues you don't have the intellect and resources to resolve" and we say to them, like Gandhi said to the British General, "that may be true, but they are *our* problems and issues, not yours." A friend from CA recently informed me that my county, Polk, in Florida is one of the poorest and least educated in the country. My response was that may be true, but we have clean air, plenty of water, little crime, $2 gasoline, lots of golf courses, affordable housing, family values, many churches and charities, we look after each other, a republican majority state government, a law-and-order sheriff, no income taxes, thousands of fresh water lakes, and beautiful beaches with warm water. We like it like that and don't need anybody from California, or any other state telling us how to live. If we could make it a liberal-free zone, we would.

Neal Gorsuch, Supreme Court Justice, said during his confirmation process, "I'm a westerner and conservative. Conservatives just want to be left alone to lead their lives as they see fit, within the bounds of the Constitution and the law," or something like that. I think all conservatives could say AMEN to that! On the other hand, liberals are constantly thinking of new ways to impose their benevolent will on the rest of the country, using other people's money, of course!

If all a person consumes is the hostile fake news of ABC, NBC, CBS, CNN, MSNBC, *Washington Post, the New York Times,* you probably think Donald Trump is the anti-Christ! But all these sources are part of the vast left-wing conspiracy, the propaganda arm of the Democratic party. They are beyond biased anymore; they are the hostile dishonest media.

This is over the top you may be thinking, how can you say these folks are bad people, they are as American as you are. Bad is a relative term and is only negative if there is a scale of some sort to place it on. Here is my scale … if what you believe, propose, insist upon, wish to impose, vote for, or desire to enforce changes my life, or others, from what it is to what you believe it should be, using other people's money … that's bad, and I'll fight you over it.

Marxist, pro-abortion, socialist liberal progressive democrat—bad!

Capitalist, pro-life Christian constitutional free-market compassionate conservative—Good!

Now, of course not all liberal democrats are commie anti-American leftists, but all such leftists are democrats, or worse. In my experience, most local democrats are well meaning but misguided Americans; some in the deep south run as democrats but vote republican, some are even friends, family members, fellow Kiwanians. Most liberal do-gooder democrats, tree huggers, and the like don't have evil black hearts; most have kind hearts. They just want a different America than conservatives do, and we are going to do everything in our power to see that they don't get their way! They wanted Hillary's America; we want Trump's America. There is no problem seeing the stark difference!

The hard-core American left, and their international communist mentors, hate the idea of America, America first, American exceptionalism, and the American dream. To the hard left, it's the American nightmare for American victims (name your favorite group) of American villains, racist descendants of slave owners, white privileged capitalist pigs, etc., you know the story … tiring, boring, exhausting 24/7. We hear how unjust, bigoted, bloated, racist, hateful, greedy, white, and sexist America is every time a democrat in congress or candidate for office opens their mouths. Despite a booming economy, record stock market, low unemployment, rising wages, cheap energy, strongest military, improved international trade prospects, and reduced job killing regulations they can't find a single good thing to say about our country, much less the president who made it happen.

It doesn't matter that not all democrats are leftists, since the leadership are all hard-core leftists and elected democrats always fall in with the party line. Same goes with communists, Muslims, Nazis, and fascist throughout history and now. Those who are not true believers but go along with the party line anyway are what Lenin and Alinsky called "useful idiots." Those who don't toe the party line are called "gone," undermined, sabotaged, entrapped, fired, or dead! Have you seen the Clinton body count lately? No one could have that many friends and associates who committed suicide or were randomly murdered!

This is typical of all leftist movements and causes over the past hundred years. They preach tolerance, but in fact once in power they are completely intolerant of speech, action, debate, or publication of anything which disagrees with their hard-left philosophy and agenda. Once ground is taken, they are jealous to protect it. Just look what is happening on college campuses today. These folks are all democrats, don't help them destroy America.

Not that republicans always get it right, they don't. Difference is that the left, manifested in politics as democrats, have been playing the long game for the last hundred years, and republicans don't seem to have game at all. Democrats stick together, play team ball, while republicans bungle along winning some losing some but with few common guiding principles the team can agree on, seems to me.

Trump is not really a Republican you know; he just knows that the two-party system is the way it is and democrats have gone so far left, his choice was easy ... so is yours if you are a patriotic, pro-life, religious, conservative who wants to Make America Great Again. Institutional Republicans are as much to blame for America's problems as the democrats. They've all been feeding at the same public trough for many decades, just alternating positions periodically, getting richer and fatter every election cycle.

CHAPTER 17
THE MAN THEY DIDN'T COUNT ON

So, what's so unique about Donald Trump's winning the presidency? Never since the founders has a person with no political or military experience won the presidency, on his first try, and by an electoral upset that shocked the media, the pundits, and the politicians, but not the public.

Not just any person, but a larger-than-life billionaire who previously was only famous for being famous ... a casino owner, Miss Universe Pageant owner, real estate mogul, builder of things like skating rinks and golf courses, reality TV star ... bankrupt, divorced, remarried several times, with an affinity for beautiful women, athlete, golfer, a man's man ... sued many times, a NY street fighter, an apolitical contributor to both sides, taught his children to drive a bulldozer and manage construction projects, fraternized with the working class, called the "Blue Collar Billionaire," a master negotiator who wrote *Art of the Deal* a business bulldog who never gives up, never gives in, never apologizes, doesn't drink or smoke, works twenty hours a day, loves burgers and fries, perfect health, incredible energy, and is obsessed with winning.

He brought those qualities to the Whitehouse after defeating seventeen republican primary challengers and then the democrats' dirty tricks machine of the DNC and Crooked Hillary Clinton. Most people don't know that the other cabal he defeated is the hard-left Shadow Party, of international socialist and open society advocate, puppet master George Soros. More on this has been discussed later.

Trump is not an establishment type or a member of the club of American elites who run everything from wall street to large corporations to big tech to universities to international banking to foreign affairs, and many of whom are secretive members of the elitist organization, the Council on Foreign Relations in NYC.

Trump made no secret of the fact that he is highly opinionated about illegal immigration, the disastrous invasion of Iraq by Bush, endless wars in the Middle East, trade deficits with Mexico, Canada, the E.U., China, loss of manufacturing jobs, need to rebuild the military, care for veterans, repeal and replace ObamaCare, disaster of NAFTA, TPP, Paris Climate Accord, Iran Nuclear Deal, unfair trade including IP theft with China, media bias, and many other things, but also pragmatic and flexible when warranted, for example, withdrawing troops from Syria despite congressional bipartisan disapproval.

Conservative Americans elected him because of these traits, not despite them. Liberal democrats, socialists, communists, and Soros hate him because he is systematically reversing the progress they made under Obama, and for the last sixty years. Easily offended anti-Trumpers across the board dislike/hate him because, like Ross Perot before, Trump is an equal opportunity offender, exudes confidence (perceived by some as arrogance), can't be bought, supports law and order, believes blue lives matter more than black lies, politically incorrect, a kick-ass-take-names businessman not a kiss-ass-play-games politician. Called a racist, sexist, xenophobe, but is not, much evidence to the contrary. His supporters labeled as irredeemable deplorables by Crooked Hillary, enjoined by the fake news media.

It is no wonder the anti-Trumpers on both sides, democrats and republicans, who have been feeding shoulder to shoulder at the same public trough for decades consider him to be an existential threat to all things "establishment" and all things "progressive." Even before the election of 2016, they determined to destroy him before he could get out of the gate, and with "a DOJ insurance policy," just in case. All their attempts have failed to stop the Trump-train and have hardly even slowed him down. They tried impeachment and that too has failed to convict and remove the president from office. These democrat shenanigans cost taxpayers tens of millions of dollars and distracted the administration from more important strategic matters, like trade negotiations, North Korea, and Iranian terrorism. They are shameful, unethical, un-American, and maybe criminal. We will know soon, when AG Barr and U.S. Attorney Durham finish their investigation!

With recent revelations in the Michael Flynn case implicating top officials, including President Obama, in a conspiracy to perjury trap General Flynn and frame Donald Trump and others, it appears the noose is tightening on the conspirators.

Any voter who approves of these activities and votes for those who do are despicable excuses for Americans. Ignorance can no longer be an excuse.

CHAPTER 18
UNCHARTED TERRITORY

We are in uncharted territory here! Never in our lifetime has the citizenry of America been so polarized, probably not since the War Between the States. As in 1865, the fate of America, and perhaps the free world, hangs in the balance and depends on what we do next. Democrats were on the wrong side of history then, and they are on the wrong side of history now!

Like Venezuela and other prosperous democracies before, we have a choice. This book is intended to provide the reader with objective information about the choices we face, with a focus on understanding a vast left-wing conspiracy, represented today at our ballot boxes by democrats. The greatest threat to the continuation of the American experiment we call the Constitutional Republic of the United States of America is not a foreign power, it is us! Like Rome, we cannot be destroyed from without, but we can fall from within. I intend to prove beyond a reasonable doubt the modern Democratic Socialist Party running against President Trump and republicans in 2020 are affiliated historically and closely related ideologically to communism.

The Soviet communists' plan for the destruction of America from within has been adopted by the modern democrat party.

The commies were at it back then, and they are still at it today … they call that progressivism. Here is a re-listing of some of their forty-five goals.

- Capture one or both political parties (give you one guess!!)

- Get control of the schools (school boards and administrations)

- Get control of teacher's associations (unions)

- Put the party line in textbooks (done)

- Infiltrate the American press (complete)

- Breakdown cultural standards of morality (60s, hippies, free love, vulgarity, obscenity, abortion, divorce)

- Present homosexuality, degeneracy, promiscuity as normal, natural, healthy (same sex marriage)

- Infiltrate and gain control of more unions (all)

- Infiltrate and gain control of big business (many, especially big tech)

- Permit free trade among all nations regardless of communist affiliation (WTO)

- Promote the UN as the only hope for mankind (constant pressure for globalism)

- Internationalize the Panama Canal (Carter did this on his watch, effective 12/31/1999)

We will list all forty-five goals in a coming chapter.

These are all now inextricably embedded in the modern democratic party. In fact, if you add a few more things even the communists couldn't imagine anyone would go for like abortion-on-demand, climate change alarmism, and open borders, the list is practically the Democratic Party Platform and Playbook. Republicans are not guilt free either. Trump is the only one who can beat them at their own game.

Some readers may read the list and say, "What's wrong with that?" I'm just pointing out that the masters-of-disaster, Soviet communists, thought these things would bring down the greatest capitalistic moral democracy in the history of the world, without firing a shot or dropping a bomb! That should give any voter pause. A vote for any democrat in 2020 is a vote for a continuation of these Soviet communist goals for the destruction of America from the inside. Liberalism and communism have the same aims and produce the same results.

They have been working their leftist agenda for many decades in the shadows, culminating in the election of a relatively unknown articulate black man with no real work history or record of accomplishments, to the highest office in the land, twice!! Go figure how that happened. Hillary Clinton was to be heir apparent to provide the coup d'état and the end of America as we've known it. But then God, and Trump, showed up!

The unlikely election of Donald Trump as President of the United States of America has provoked the left to desperation, to come out of the closet, to fight in the open. The media, which used to be respectfully referred to as "biased" but "free" press, are now openly hostile to conservative values and President Trump and are called the fake news in derision. President Trump has been so effective in his job that the left has nothing positive to run on in 2020, no new ideas, no accomplishments. Their only hope is to destroy him in the media and public opinion with bogus charges of collusion, obstruction, treason … or worse, maybe a pandemic, or recession which they can deliberately exacerbate!

The Russian witch hunt and impeachment inquiry was a three-ring circus for all the world to see. All the democratic leaders look like the clown brigade. When the Inspector General's report, unredacted documents, and the John Durham investigation comes out, the democrats will rue the day they ever opened this can of worms, I predict … we'll soon see.

Now is the right time to expose their Marxist/communist/socialist roots for all to see. Democrats seem to be self-confessing their socialist preferences. I'll help get the word out for them in this book!

Throughout our history, other candidates have been opposed by groups and individuals outside government who did not believe they represented their best interests or values and that's just the American political system, but what makes this situation unique is that this time the elites outside government had inside help from the FBI, CIA, NSA, IRS, DOJ, EPA, and other powerful agencies in the Obama administration. In fact, it is perhaps the case that the insiders were in the lead, not just being helpful. That's because Obama had purged and replanted these agencies, including the Pentagon, CIA, and FBI with his own ilk during the eight years of his reign.

These people of the deep state, allied with the NGOs of the Shadow Party, a leftist cabal created by George Soros to defeat George Bush in 2004, have made taking out this president of the United States their new life and death priority. Since I believe that Obama was a Marxist-inspired, Muslim-loving, racist bigot whose goal seems to have been to cripple America so that it could never be great again, it is not unrealistic to believe his appointees on critical intelligence, regulatory, administrative, and law enforcement agencies could serve his purposes even after he left office. In fact, Obama himself, a type of "Manchurian Candidate," is a product of a larger scheme that dates back to the mid-twentieth century to take down

America and replace ("fundamentally transform" to use Obama's words) it with a utopian socialist society.

We are in a mess, maybe even a constitutional crisis ... but, how did we get here? How could this happen to America, a constitutional republic, a "shining city on a hill" as Reagan put it? It began in Europe with Karl Marx in the mid-nineteenth century. It began in America in the early twentieth century with the socialist philosophy that emerged from the Russian Revolution being introduced to America.

CHAPTER 19
COMMUNISM COMES TO AMERICA

Soviet socialism, as an organizing principle for social justice, was admired by many American intellectuals, press, and politicians. Lenin, and later Stalin, welcomed their support, but knowing they were not true revolutionaries willing to do whatever is necessary, called them "useful idiots." That's what many unwitting democrats, politicians, and voters, are today.

Reagan once said the if communism ever comes to America, it will come in the form of liberalism.

David Horowitz's Jewish parents were two of those liberal card-carrying, but passive law-abiding communists who resided in Queens, NY, in the early twentieth century awaiting the establishment of a Soviet-style state in America ... go figure! Many others were in Chicago, LA/Hollywood, San Francisco, DC, and other American cities. The commies in America, under orders and with support from Moscow, infiltrated the government, academia, Hollywood, the press, the Church, and even the Manhattan Project.

Another old commie, on the FBI watch list, was Frank Marshall Davis. "Frank" was a friend of Barry Soetoro's grandfather and mentor to young Barry while he lived in Hawaii. He must have had influence since Barry, aka Barak, stated in his book, "When in college, I sought out the Marxist professors and radical students." Obama attended Occidental College in CA and then Columbia University in NY, both hotbeds of communist activity in that day; he did not have to look far.

When it comes to left-wing politics, one university stands alone, Columbia University, has been a training ground for America-hating radicals since at least the start of the twentieth century. The left has had to take new direction since the collapse of the Soviet Union in 1991, but before that leftists' scholars from Columbia often expressed their loathing for the American way by supporting Soviet-centered communism.

Obama attended Columbia from 1981–83, then went to Harvard in 1988 for a law degree. Reagan was president from 1981–89. While Reagan was fighting to destroy communism from the White House, a young Obama was soaking it up at Columbia and Harvard. Who could have imagined this good looking, articulate, young black communist sympathizer would someday sit in the same Oval office as Ronald Reagan and come very close to achieving a long held communist goal to fatally wound America so that it could never be great again?

By the mid-twentieth century, the Roosevelt administration was shot through with card carrying Soviet communists and communist sympathizers. Alger Hiss, a primary author of the UN Charter after WW2 was later revealed to be a Soviet communist spy. Harry Dexter White enrolled at Columbia in 1922 and would go on to become one of the most influential Soviet agents in the Roosevelt and Truman Administration, attending the Bretton Woods conference where the World Bank and the International Monetary Fund were founded. In 1925 a former Columbia student named Whittaker Chambers joined the Communist Party (CP) and in 1932 Chambers began his career as a senior Soviet spy. Eventually he would renounce Communism and give the names of dozens of his fellow spies to the FBI. He wrote a book, *Witness*, about his life and times. Elizabeth Bentley, successor to Chambers, joined the CP in 1935 while working on a master's degree at Columbia. In 1945, she repented and began cooperating with J. Edgar Hoover's FBI. A young actor and president of the Screen Actors Guild found out communists had infiltrated the organization and resigned. His name was Ronald Reagan, and hence began Reagan's crusade to understand and defeat the scourge of communism. Reagan, a former democrat, switched to the republican party in 1962 and supported Barry Goldwater for president in 1964, having become a conservative by then. Reagan associated the democratic party with communist ideology. He had also heard and read W. Cleon Skousen's *The Naked Communist*.

Many world leaders and historians credit the Reagan Doctrine, reversing the Nixon and Carter administration's policy of Détente, as having been the key to the end of the Cold War and the dissolution of Soviet Union in 1991. The Soviet Union of socialist republics may have crumbled under its own weight, but communism is still alive and well in the world. There is no longer a need for a Communist party in the U.S. as the democrats have adopted all their forty-five goals, plus some, for the destruction of America from the inside. But why would they do this, you ask? Keep reading.

If they were honest, which they are not, their party motto should just be "Repeal and Replace America," the title of this book! Proposals for America's replacement are flowing freely from all the democrat candidates for president, but they will need to first repeal what it is. For example, before they can replace health care with Medicare-for-All, they would need to repeal private health care. Burn down or overwhelm the system first, because no one would voluntarily choose government-run health care if they could keep their company-paid plans. Obama lied to get his plan passed; they make no pretense anymore … private health care violates all good socialist principles and must go; for the good of the many, the few must conform.

An excerpt from the Wikipedia definition of democratic socialism, discussed in detail in a later chapter, this is a profound statement and cuts to the heart of what democrats believe today.

> *Democratic Socialists believe the fundamental issues with capitalism are systemic in nature and can only be resolved by replacing the capitalist economic system with socialism, i.e., by* (repealing and) *replacing private ownership with collective ownership of the means of production and extending democracy to the economic sphere.*

I don't believe that you say ... well, the democrat socialist party does, so don't vote them into power! Don't be one of their useful idiots.

In the 50s, Senator Joseph McCarthy, leading an investigation on "Un-American Activities," was discredited, by the left and the media, and we still cringe at being accused of McCarthyism. Joe, a former combat marine, may have been overly aggressive, but he was right! Joe McCarthy managed to expose and get rid of much of the communist influence in the government and Hollywood, but that just drove them underground for a time.

CHAPTER 20
THE LEFT GOES UNDERGROUND

One of the leading commie activists of that day Saul Alinsky said, "Few of us survived the Joe McCarthy holocaust of the early 50s and of those there were even fewer whose understanding and insights had developed beyond the dialectical materialism of orthodox Marxism." Alinsky set out to fix that problem.

In 1971, Alinsky wrote and published the new-left's handbook, *Rules for Radicals: A Pragmatic Primer for Realistic Radicals*," that would guide a new generation of leftist activists such as Hillary Clinton and Barak Obama. Alinsky advised, out with the bomb throwing of Obama's friend and fellow traveler Bill Ayers, out with riots by the SDS, out with murders by the Black Panthers, and in with the "patient infiltration and organizing of every institution to subvert every element of society from the inside." Ayers, a rich spoiled hippie, who barely escaped prison for killing a police office, cut his hair and went to college. He is now professor of English at the University of Chicago and is still a close friend of Obama.

After "seeking out Marxist professors and radical students" at Occidental and Columbia, Obama got a law degree from Harvard and then joined his old friend Bill Ayers and his rich father, CEO of Con Edison Utilities, in Chicago to learn the "Chicago Way" of politics. He sat for many years at the feet of the America hating, anti-Semitic, white bashing, Louis Farrakhan praising, Black Liberation Theology preaching Reverend Jerimiah Wright, remember him "God bless America, no I say God Damn America."

The holocaust of McCarthyism, as Alinsky put it, simply drove the new-left commies underground to plot their next moves. They would reemerge in the 60s, spring boarding off the civil rights, War on Poverty, and Great Society movements and into the Vietnam War era protest movement ... not a peace movement, a communist backed anti-American movement.

Democrat politicians in Congress succumbed to pressure and pulled all support from South Vietnam after we had won the war. Over 2 million Vietnamese, Cambodians, and Laotians were murdered by communists in the "Killing Fields" left behind by our retreat. It would have been the same in Korea had we withdrawn completely. American communists and the democrats declared victory but spit on our soldiers when they returned home.

Swift Boat John Kerry was one of those accusing our soldiers of war crimes, not mentioning the atrocities committed by the communists against their own people. Being dumped for president, Kerry would have his revenge on America by negotiating the disastrous Iran Nuclear Deal for the Obama administration, essentially financing a new generation of Middle East terrorism for Iran. This also suited the needs of the Soros' open society agenda to keep the chaos and death going. Peace and stability, especially security for Israel is the worst thing that could happen for Soros and his ilk.

The left was ecstatic, European socialist countries were giddy, Obama got reelected ... but then along came Trump! BAM!!! And just like that no more Iran Deal, no more Paris Climate Accord, no more TPP, no more NAFTA, no more China ripping us off, no more depleted military, no more mistreatment of veterans at the VA, no more high taxes, no more excessive job-killing regulations, no more free rides for NATO, no more open borders, no more apologies for the United States ... all these and much much more accrue to the detriment of the left's agenda for the fundamental transformation of American from what it is to what they believe it should be … and they hate Trump and his deplorable supporters for it!

Remember the game Dungeons and Dragons, well the left's go-to game today is Victims and Villains. It's their favorite tactic to convert naive useful idiots into committed revolutionary zealots. The low hanging fruit for justified activism was legitimate injustices like slavery, segregation, workers' rights, women's rights, environmental pollution, etc., all of which are mostly solved or under control. The left is still stirring those pots, fanning those flames, but new victims and villains must be found to keep the money moving and the power shifting. Examples are climate change, wealth inequality, open borders, and the green new deal to name a few.

There are plenty of current books and videos and even movies out on the deep state, the shadow government, Trump's enemies, secret empires, power grab, the Russia hoax, exonerated, etc. by great authors like Newt Gingrich, Dinesh DeSousa, Heather MacDonald, Dan Bongino, Peter Schweitzer, Victor David Hanson, Greg Garret, and others, and I've read most of them. I will use a lot of their wisdom and facts in this book, but I'm most interested in the books from a previous time like:

- *The Communist Manifesto,* by Karl Marx and Frederick Engels, 1848.

- *The Naked Communist,* by W. Cleon Skousen, 1958.

- *Rules for Radicals: A Pragmatic Primer for Realistic Radicals,* by Saul Alinsky, 1971.

- *The Vast Left-Wing Conspiracy: The Untold Story of How the Democratic Operatives, Eccentric Billionaires, Liberal Activists, and Assorted Celebrated Celebrities Tried to Bring Down a President (GW Bush), and Why They'll Try Even Harder Next Time,* by Byron York, 2005.

- *The Shadow Party: How George Soros, Hillary Clinton, and Sixties Radicals Seized Control of the Democratic Party*, by David Horowitz and Richard Poe, 2006

CHAPTER 21
VAMPIRE KILLERS

Communist leaders are like vampires; from the first of their kind, Karl Marx, in the mid-1800s, they just keep coming out of the grave to suck the blood out of the next generation. Our goal should be to drive a red, white, and blue stake with Keep America Great on it through their black hearts, burn the cross of Christianity into their rotten foreheads, cut off their retreat to the underground until exposure to sunlight destroys their ability to function, then block their kind's reemergence from hell for at least a generation, until the millennials and students, who they have glamoured unconscious, come to their senses!

A bit of hyperbole here but it does paint a graphic and realistic picture! Sound daunting, impossible? Not so, just think what getting one more conservative Justice on the Supreme Court would mean—conservatives would be six and liberals would be three. We only need to reelect Trump, the Vampire Killer, and keep a majority in the Senate, and regain a House majority for that to happen.

I hate to think what well-funded leftists like George Soros may be prepared to do to prevent it from happening. Their kind have been willing to pull strings that caused millions to die in the past, e.g., end of the Vietnam war—one life would mean nothing to them. The end justifies the means.

What kind of take-down hit job would a billion dollars buy? Soros said he'd give his whole fortune to prevent G.W. Bush being reelected in 2004, "if it would guarantee it!" I believe the Shadow Party, likely ordered Obama, their Manchurian Candidate, to execute a shadow government/deep state frame job on Trump and it failed. What shall it be this time? A plan with a more certain outcome, I fear.

The first comprehensive book on Trump was written by hostile journalists from *the Washington Post* in 2016 before the election. It was called "Trump Revealed" and it was a major disappointment to the left and the media because there was no mud to sling, no skeletons in Trumps closet. He has always been an open-source philanderer, playboy, wheeler dealer, hard ball player, aggressive businessman ... i.e., it's all old news. The next book, after Trump is reelected should be called *Trump Unleashed*, because that is what he will be, and the left knows it. To the communists and other America First haters, inside and outside our government, failure is not an option this time around. Many thought Trump could not take the storm of investigations and obstruction and personal insults they threw at him, but not to worry ... Trump says, "Bring it, I AM THE STORM"!

CHAPTER 22
COMMUNISTS AND CONSERVATIVES

This chapter will identify the issues, activities, and groups the left uses to advance their agenda of transforming America from what it is to what they believe it should be.

A former radical lefty from the 50s and 60s, David Horowitz, says that when he left the left and sought out conservative brothers to join, he couldn't find any. Conservatives had no ground game to join! He said that leftist activist, like he was, think about politics 24/7. They wake up every morning contemplating what they could do that day to further their cause of the day. Even if they must go to work, they are thinking about it, planning, plotting, subverting. That's why they are called "activists," I suppose, it's their life.

On the other hand, conservatives have a real life, typically with as little politics in them as absolutely necessary … they work hard, raise their children, obey the law, go to school to learn, go to church to worship, enjoy friends and family, explore nature, and have hobbies like fishing, hunting, golf. I used to wonder if all those protestors I saw on TV in the 60s and 70s took precious vacation time off (I had two weeks/year) and used their savings (I had more bills and tuition than savings) to attend those rallies … how naïve, right? I've since learned that most such leftist "rallies" are paid for by the likes of George Soros and those sponsors and activists he recruits.

Conservatives don't protest and go to rallies typically, they are not activist, they have lives, they have better things to do. But the Trump phenomenon has brought conservatives out in droves, standing online for hours or even days to get into a Trump rally. The tea party could draw a crowd in its day, but it never had a charismatic bombastic leader like Trump. Not since P.T. Barnum and Teddy Roosevelt has America seen anyone like Trump. Something new and different is going on; it's an awakening of sorts, almost religious in nature. Politics in a post-Trump world will never be the same. No longer are conservatives going to just bend over and take it. Deplorables of the world unite!

So, what is a leftist anyway? First, not all democrats are leftists, but all leftists today are democrats. I used to say "... or worse." No need to say that anymore because the democratic party of today has embraced the best of both communist and socialist philosophies and call it democratic socialism. No need for a communist or socialist candidate for office anymore. They haven't fully embraced anarchy and revolution yet but it's probably just around the corner, especially if Trump wins in 2020. Antifa and Black Lies Matter being an exception and perhaps a precursor of things to come. Back in the day of the 60s, it was Black Panthers (Huey Newton), the SDS (Tom Hayden), the Weather Underground (Bill Ayers group), and other violent and subversive radical groups. Before that the KKK was the militant arm of the party ... democrats all!

Saul Alinsky, in 1971, admonished his readers of *Rules for Radicals* to abandon tactics which expose their true agenda and just alienates people but rather to *organize for action* to create mass organizations to seize power and give it to the people. From this new-left philosophy came students like a young Hillary Clinton and later Barak Obama, both admirers of Alinsky and his "community organizing" approach instead of violence which could be defeated by powerful authorities. Not so coincidentally,

> *"Organizing for Action today is a 501(c)(4) nonprofit organization and community organizing project that advocates for the agenda of former US President Barack Obama, the organization is officially non-partisan, but its agenda and policies are strongly allied with the Democratic Party."* —*Wikipedia.*

Its unofficial headquarters is Obama's Washington DC compound and mansion very near the capital. Funding is provided by a who's who of American and international leftists who do not have traditional American values in mind.

Then, what are some of the causes the left obsesses over? First let's a look at the founding principles and key strategies. The first line in the *Communist Manifesto* is, "The history of all hitherto existing society is one of class struggles." Marx divided the society he knew into bourgeois and proletarians.

> "By Bourgeois is meant people in the class of modern capitalists, owners of the means of social production and employers of wage labor. By Proletarians, the people in the class of modern wage laborers who, having no means of production of their own, are reduced to selling their labor power in order to live."

Marx saw this division as patently unfair, much the way Warren and Sanders see income and wealth inequality as unfair. Both create a narrative that "something must be done." This is a pillar of religion of the left ... that there is a major problem, caused by class struggle, one group are the villains, the other are the victims of social, financial, environmental injustice. The "problem" which must be solved by urgent coercive government action, may be real, perceived, created, or just made up and sold as real ... like anthropogenic global warming, now referred to as climate change.

CHAPTER 23
CLIMATE CHANGE—WEAPONIZING THE WEATHER

This is a subject of enormous impact and consequences. Trillions of dollars are at stake, governments and entire economies could fall, and human displacement and famine could escalate into global war. But NOT because the climate is changing abnormally, producing catastrophic consequences, because it's not, and will not. Our misguided overreaction to "climate change," is what could trigger catastrophic and cataclysmic upsets in economies, demographics, and social functioning. This is exactly what the left wants, large scaled upsets in social functioning…burn it down, overwhelm it, destroy it. The Paris Climate Accord and the Green New Deal would be the Mother-of-all-Bombs on our economy and way of life, quickly creating an apocalyptic scene in America from which we may never recover. That would be just fine for Soros, Obama, Clinton, Bernie, Pelosi and their ilk who would be above the fray to transform the chaos into utopia… the goal of all communists for the last hundred years. I didn't include Biden in the list above because he is just a puppet, not having the intellect or presence of mind to even hatch or execute a good plot and scheme. He doesn't know what he believes, hell … he doesn't even know where he is half the time. I didn't include AOC because she is just a dumb, ignorant, useful idiot – nay – just an idiot!

The left believes that wealth inequality, power inequality, and status inequality across the planet is immoral and unacceptable. George Soros' vision for the world is a classless, borderless, stateless open society where all resources are shared by all people, to be distributed by one benevolent organization ... the UN at first, then eliminating the UN, and passing the torch to a central authority like the World Bank perhaps. But what does that have to do with climate change?

To the far-left, like Soros, Sanders, Warren, and UN bureaucrats, the industrialized highly developed capitalist nations are the villains, and the underdeveloped nations of the world are the victims. They believe, or feign to believe, if they could just cripple the villains and move most of their resources and power to the victims, world equality could be achieved. Sounds scary, absurd, onerous! It is, and that's why they would never put it that way.

But what if they could find a way to find or create a problem so monumental, gain worldwide consensus of its apocalyptic global consequences, and propose an easily understood solution so broad that it would accomplish their goals without the public even realizing what they were doing.

The problem they, and Al Gore, cooked up originally was global warming. The mother of all leftist causes today is what they call now "Climate Change." In fact, the earth has been warming gradually since the middle of the Little Ice Age several hundred years ago, but not smoothly. Statistically, there has been no significant warming for the last twenty years despite many ups and down, and even a few "record highs." The cause of global warming, they identified uniquely, is atmospheric CO_2, now erroneously referred to as carbon pollution. CO_2 is the only factor among dozens of other more significant influences that they can arguably blame on human behavior ... perfect for forcing societal change!

Over the past forty years or so, the left has duped practically the entire world into believing that CO_2 is the primary cause of global warming, and that global warming shall lead to catastrophic climate change on a grand scale … and most importantly, unless we immediately begin to rapidly and urgently "decarbonize" the planet, our years are numbered … to only a few more years, twelve at the most.

Al Gore recently stated that "Decarbonization of the planet should be the organizing principle of all civilized nations in this century" or something like that. They say that since a consensus of 97 percent of the world's climate scientists agree, the science is settled, and no skepticism, challenges, or denials shall be allowed, under penalty of ridicule, career destruction, grant withdrawals, even riots and revolts. They have even enlisted ignorant school children to their cause now.

Bill Gates says we must get to zero carbon emissions by reducing human population, the services the population uses, the type of energy the population uses, and the activities the population engages in. He says CO2 is the primary cause of global warming and that global warming, if not stopped, will produce catastrophic climate change. Gates knows a lot about some things but on this subject, he is way off the mark and completely out of his wheelhouse. To follow his advice would produce a return to the stone age, at least the horse and buggy days. He is spreading dangerous falsehoods to naïve people who respect his opinion. I no longer do!

I can write with credibility on this subject, because of my long, broad, and deep career and education in science, technology, engineering, and math (STEM). I'm able to read and understand all the science, and the politics, related to climate science. Bill Gates is wrong. Dr. Lindzen and thousands of other eminent scientists are right. Climate change alarmism caused by "Global Warming is about politics and power rather than science. In science there is an attempt to clarify; in global warming, language is misused in order to confuse and mislead the public." —Richard S. Lindzen, PhD Atmospheric Physics, MIT. He is one of the most esteemed climate scientists in the world today. I am disappointed to hear Bill Gates going so public about something he apparently knows little about. His wealth and power do not entitle him to preach lies and globalism to an unsuspecting public. Shame on you, Bill.

More from Dr. Richard Lindzen:

> "The advocates frame the issue in terms of yes–no answers to questions they propose, for example:

- Does climate change?

- Is carbon dioxide (CO2) a greenhouse gas?

- Does adding greenhouse gases cause 'warming'?

- Can man's activities cause increases in greenhouse gases?

These yes–no questions are meaningless when it comes to global warming alarmism since affirmative answers are still completely consistent with there being no problem whatsoever; crucial to the scientific method are 'how much' questions."

The solution they proposed was reducing fossil fuel emissions of CO2 to some arbitrary level in order to limit surface temperature rise to another arbitrary level. They also assured us that catastrophic weather events, forest fires, sea level rise, population displacement, death and destruction of human and animal life would follow if we did not act immediately.

There is no credible evidence of correlation between surface air temperature changes of plus or minus a couple of degrees and any of these events and some are even inverted, e.g., drought is caused by regional lack of rainfall which produces hot dry conditions, not the other way around. Warmer weather evaporates more liquid water and makes more clouds. Water vapor is the primary greenhouse gas (96 percent) and clouds have an unpredictably positive and negative effect on temperature. It rains most every day in the middle of the summer in Florida. The worst storms and destructive weather in the North are during the coldest months, etc.

It is beyond the scope of this book to prove or disprove the man-induced global warming hypothesis pushed by the UN and the left for their own political purposes. But I can assure the reader there are thousands of credible scientists, not on the government or academic dole, who are skeptical of the UN's Intergovernmental Panel on Climate Change's (IPCC's) conclusions.

Climate Change is their best example of perfect sequencing by the left. Here's how they pulled it off. Working through the UN, who established the IPCC, the left first perpetrated the "fact" of *abnormal* global warming, then blamed it on man-caused CO2 emissions, ignoring the many natural non-man-induced factors contributing to the climate, or acknowledging the earth has been gradually warming since coming out of the Little Ice Age which bottomed out around 1700 AD. Then they manipulated historical data to make it look like the last seventy-five years are unprecedented and all the recent warming must be coming from CO2 emissions from burning fossil fuels since the industrial boom post World War II.

Then they touted a misleading poll that "97 percent consensus of all climate scientists agrees with Mann's hockey stick diagram and conclusions." Then they tweaked their models to predict excessive rise in global temperature correlated with rising CO2 levels. Then they projected catastrophic consequences like storms, wildfires, sea level rise, glacial melting, extinction of species, etc. Then they asserted with "Extreme Confidence" that if the world did not curtail emissions of CO2 within the next decade, a tipping point would be reached, a point of no return. The pundits, the press, the politicians, and sixteen-year-old Greta Thunberg declared the world would not survive another twelve years. OH MY GOD!!!! HOW DARE YOU!!!! SOMETHING MUST BE DONE!!!!

Very sophisticated, very effective ... selling climate change alarmism is the most successful of the left's attempts to manipulate human behavior to achieve their goals of global egalitarianism, bring down the haves, by transferring wealth and power to the have-nots. Soros was highly gratified. Well, he was back then, now he's mortified ... by Trump!

So, here is where the consensus claim comes from:

> "It derives from a survey sent to 10,257 people with a self-interest in human-induced global warming who published 'science' supported by taxpayer-funded research grants. Replies from 3,146 respondents were whittled down to 77 self-appointed climate 'scientists' of whom 75 were judged to agree that human-induced warming was taking place. The 97 percent figure thus derives from a dataset with only 75 members. But 75 is actually 2.38 percent of those who responded, and only 0.73 percent of all those polled, not 97 percent. Only a small fraction of those with a self-interest who agreed that humans have played a significant role in changing climate *and* that are recipients of some of the billions spent annually on climate research were counted." — Ian Plimer, Emeritus Professor of Earth Sciences at University of Melbourne.

In the author's scientific (applied physics, analytical chemistry, data analytics, computer science) opinion, global warming alarmism leading to catastrophic climate change due to fossil fuel emissions of $CO2$ is a deliberate scientific fraud, a leftist political hoax, and a globalist financial scam of monumental proportions. Despite the well-known climate influences of dozens of more naturally occurring highly significant factors, like water vapor, clouds, solar activity, etc., the UN's IPCC mandated that their policy makers focus on only human-caused factors, and $CO2$ drew the short straw.

You must understand the goals and tactics of the left to fathom how they could possibly use something like weather trends to their advantage. Remember they always first think … burn the system down, then rebuild utopia upon the ashes. Therefore, the "cause" of the "effect" had to have a human fingerprint, or footprint, on it. CO_2 was deemed the most impactful of the candidates, but they would need to cook up some evidence, discredit the historical data, reconstruct new data, build models to suit their desired conclusions, and then get the media and member states to hype it up, until the cry "something must be done" was deafening … screamed by scientists who should know better, bureaucrats who did know better, and even school children who don't know anything.

Complying with the Paris Climate Accord would have crippled America's economy and given China, India, and Russia significant advantage over us at many levels. This would have been in alignment with Obama's goal to cripple America so that it could never be great again. And, with Soros' goal to create what he calls an open society, a classless, borderless world where all people share all resources, to be confiscated and redistributed fairly by a single central benevolent authority. Soros is the ultimate socialist, no one else even comes close. We are fortunate he is already eighty years old and looks like walking death. He is an avowed atheist, but he won't be much longer.

Atmospheric Physicist Richard Lindzen, PhD, of MIT and the most respected living climate scientist on earth says,

> *"What historians will definitely wonder about in future centuries is how deeply flawed logic, obscured by shrewd and unrelenting propaganda, actually enabled a coalition of powerful special interests to convince nearly everyone in the world that CO2 from human industry was a dangerous planet-destroying toxin. It will be remembered as the greatest mass delusion in the history of the world— that CO2, the life of plants, was considered for a time to be a deadly poison."*

Ian Plimer—Emeritus Professor of Earth Sciences at the University of Melbourne says,

> "The theory of human-induced global warming is not science because it is based on a pre-ordained conclusion, huge bodies of evidence are ignored, and the analytical procedures are treated as evidence. Furthermore, climate 'science' is sustained by government research grants. Funds are not available to investigate theories that are not in accord with government ideology."

And then here are what 31,487 scientists like the author, including 9,029 PhDs have signed, called the Petition Project. The organizers said they could have gotten thousands more but ran out of stamps!

> See www.petitionproject.org for details.

> *"We urge the United States government to reject the global warming agreement that was written in Kyoto, Japan in December 1997, and any other similar proposals. The proposed limits on greenhouse gases would harm the environment, hinder the advance of science and technology, and damage the health and welfare of mankind.*

> *There is no convincing scientific evidence that human release of carbon dioxide, methane, or other greenhouse gases is causing, or will in the foreseeable future, cause catastrophic heating of the Earth's atmosphere and disruption of the Earth's climate. Moreover, there is substantial evidence that increases in atmospheric carbon dioxide produce many beneficial effects upon the natural plant and animal environments of the Earth."*

The fact that most scientists on the government or academic dole of grants and tenure disagree with those above reinforces my case, not diminishes it. The left is united in pushing its agenda for more control and power over every aspect of our lives, and control over the climate agenda is the mother of all leverages.

Regarding the last statement about CO2, I've learned the following: prior to the industrial age CO2 concentration was declining steadily for centuries and had reached a level of 180 ppm. Plants photosynthesize CO2 to produce what they need to grow, and discharge oxygen (O2) in the process. Animals do just the opposite, we metabolize O2 with digestible food and breath out CO2. Any credible botanist will tell you that plants die when CO2 concentration gets to less than 130–150 ppm, i.e., we were on a path to total extinction of plant life on earth ... and when all the plants die all the animals quickly follow. So, just in time, mankind unwittingly began to return some of the sequestered carbon to the atmosphere as CO2 by burning carbon-based 'fossil' fuels, making cement, and other industrial age processes ... $C + O_2 = CO_2 + heat\ energy$. We converted the heat energy to mechanical energy (steam engines, automobiles) and later electrical energy (coal to steam to electricity) to power an industrial revolution which brought mankind out of the horse and buggy days where he had existed for thousands of years into the modern era of lighting, heating, air conditioning, trains, planes, and automobiles, steel, aluminum, concrete, etc.

Who wants to go back to the good old days? AOC and the squad, and many democrats, that's who! They call it "The Green New Deal." However, to their chagrin, an unforeseen benefit to burning fossil fuel which produces CO2 is the re-greening of the planet, a fact which has be shown by satellite photos. Following their desires would produce the "Brown Old Deal" again. A return to the Brown Old Deal would serve leftists purposes to burn down the existing economy and institutions, to give them a chance to rebuild a utopia of their own dreams. True progressive revolutionaries like Obama, Clinton, Pelosi, Schumer know this, useful idiots like AOC are just well, idiots! The Paris Climate Accord would have produced the Brown Old Deal also.

For the skeptics out there, be it known that hot house farmers and industrial size plant factories all increase the CO2 concentration in their closed environment to around 1200 ppm, the optimum for faster larger growing plants requiring less water. Current atmospheric CO2 is around 400 ppm. So, you want a greener planet that requires less water to grow vegetation, fewer food shortages, fewer drought impacts, more oxygen, burn more fossil fuels, and use more concrete! To see a credible scientist telling this story himself, YouTube Patrick Moore. He was a co-founder of Greenpeace, the only one with a science background, PhD. They originally stopped the testing of hydrogen bombs in the atmosphere, disrupted industrial whaling by Japan and USSR and killing baby seals for their furs but then Greenpeace took a radical turn in the 70s and Dr. Moore left them to find out what he was *for* instead of what he was *against*. For your information, he is a big proponent of clean safe nuclear power, and a big opponent of global warming alarmism, erroneously called climate change. I agree with all his positions.

The United States did not sign the Kyoto Protocol, but that did not stop the advocates. They returned to the fight and through UN bureaucrats, false science, and political maneuvering, produced the Paris Climate Accord, which our president, Obama, did sign. This committed the United States, but not China, Russia, or India, to specific reductions in CO2 emissions by date certain. It also called for the wealthy "polluting" nations, meaning the U.S., to provide a transfer of huge amounts of money to undeveloped nations, like China and India, really!!!

Complying with this accord would have crippled the U.S. economy, industry, transportation, agriculture, energy, and military. Obama was licking his lips at this prospect. He was going to take the U.S. to its knees where he feels it belongs after two hundred years of egregious transgressions against mankind and mother earth; finally, social, economic, and environmental justice was going to become his legacy to the world ... well, that and financing his Muslim brothers in Iran to continue their jihad against America and Israel. But then along came Trump, and just like that … no more Paris Climate Accord or Iran Nuke Deal. Decades of shrewd manipulation and propaganda went down the tubes. So, the Manchurian Candidate, who was raised by communists and Muslims, and his handlers were stopped cold, for now!

President Trump wisely withdrew the U.S. from the Paris Climate Accord and the Iran Nuclear Deal early in his presidency.

Our local TV weatherman recently said at a Kiwanis presentation,

> "We can't even accurately predict the local weather or the path of a hurricane three days from now, and we sure as hell can't predict the climate thirty years from now." But based on inconclusive evidence, debatable science, and policy bias, the commie/socialist/left want us to give up cheap, plentiful energy because a bunch of UN bureaucrats and globalist politicians say so. Adoption of the UN demands, the Paris Climate Accords, or the Green New Deal would be tantamount to committing economic suicide for America … something Obama and his comrades in the Democratic Socialist Party would love to see and "then upon the ashes they could build a utopian society of social and environment justice for all."

If you want to believe in man-induced (anthropogenic) global warming and live in fear of a resulting cataclysm, that's your business. But if you want the rest of us to fundamentally change our lifestyles to accommodate your paranoia, you've now made it our business! You'll need to have more conclusive evidence for the necessity of doing so than is currently the case. Learn the facts, don't be duped, consider the sources … don't be a "useful idiot" for the left.

CHAPTER 24
CHARLES DARWIN—WHY THE ORIGIN OF LIFE MATTERS

Most will know that Karl Marx is the father of communism, and that Charles Darwin proposed the theory of evolution of species, but what do they have in common, and why should we care? It turns out that these two men, who both lived and did their work in the middle of the nineteenth century, are arguably the most influential in modern history … and not in a good way! Their role in our story of why the left wants to repeal and replace America, preferring socialism over capitalism, is foundational.

In my scientific opinion, the next major "consensus" to fall is going to be godless undirected biological evolution of species, as Darwin describes it. This is bucking the consensus … of probably every biologist, but not every scientist. Remember physics is the fundamental science, to which even chemistry and biology must conform! Evolutionary biology does not conform, and as hard as they've tried, neither biologists nor chemists have been able to produce anything even close to a single cell. For any scientific theory to be taken seriously, eventually other scientists must be able to reproduce your claims with documented results and data. Dr. James Tour (see him on YouTube), a renowned synthetic organic chemist says, "With all the science and technology available today, biological evolution as a theory has not made any progress for 50 years. That's because perhaps they are barking up the wrong tree!"

Darwin did the best he could with what he had, given the state of science in his day, but that was a long time ago! Not knowing about molecular biology, nanoscale machines, synthetic organic chemistry, DNA, or big data statistics, and information theory, Darwin in the mid-nineteenth century described what he could observe and extrapolated the rest. His observations seemed to indicate an undirected process of random mutations and natural selection of traits like beak length, size, fur color, etc. Even Darwin admitted he could describe the *survival* of the fittest within a species but could not explain the *arrival* of the fittest of a species … but that did not preclude him crafting his famous "tree-of-life" showing apparent transition from species to species, by undirected natural selection and the monkey to man picture still in textbooks today. Acknowledging the lack of a fossil record for intermediate species, he basically went forth anyway, postulating that "well, someday we will discover them," but we haven't! His proposition was inductive reasoning and speculation, not hard science. Inductive reasoning is primarily concerned with making generalizations that are broad and these are based on specific observations. This is the opposite of deductive reasoning, the basis of real science. Darwin made many "observations," but his conclusions were generalizations, i.e., that survival of the fittest could explain the evolution to entirely new genetic species and body plans. That may be because Darwin was not a physical scientist at all. He was a medical school dropout who studied rocks and animals as a "naturalist." That's a fancy word for a nature aficionado without a degree in science. Pre-dating Einstein, his, and Marx's, worldview presumed the preexistence of the universe, the oceans, and the "primordial soup" of chemicals which would somehow miraculously coalesce to form the first living cell. According to Darwin, from that first amorphous plug of chemical protoplasm all life on earth developed. Some early evolutionary biologists called this ectoplasm, like the goo from *Ghostbusters*, not the highly structured, complex, bio-mechanical, code-controlled, membrane-contained protein factory we know it to be today. Then they say somehow all simple and complex life on earth just evolved, on its own, giving the appearance of design, but not designed at all. According to Darwin, given enough time and enough random mutations, anything is possible, and while the vast majority of mutations would not improve life, and would in fact be fatal, natural selection would guide a chain of events which would lead to human life as we know it today. Physics, information theory, and probability theory do not support his claims today.

I've always considered this proposition to be archaic, absurd, and unsupportable by evidence, real science, and common sense. In my educated contrarian opinion, Darwin's theory of biological evolution is a relic of a past macro-scientific generation who didn't understand, or could even imagine, microscale and nanoscale molecular biology or digital information theory.

CHAPTER 25
ET MEETS DNA: THE SEARCH FOR EXTRATERRESTRIAL LIFE

From the NASA website:

"Since the beginning of civilization, people have wondered if we are alone in the universe or whether there is intelligent life somewhere else. In the late twentieth century, scientists converged upon the basic idea of scanning the sky and 'listening' for non-random patterns of electromagnetic emissions such as radio or television waves in order to detect another possible civilization somewhere else in the universe. In late 1959 and early 1960, the modern SETI era began when Frank Drake conducted the first such SETI search at approximately the same time that Giuseppe Cocconi and Philip Morrison published a key journal article suggesting this approach."

In short, SETI was looking for "signals," intelligent coded information, embedded in electromagnetic radiation (microwaves) from outer space that would meet information theory's definition of being "unnatural" or intelligently designed, by beings like us, e.g., morse code with a message humanly meaningful, or like the instructions on how to build a machine to travel through space and time, as in the movie *Contact* or the code for building complex self-reproducing nanomachines, like living cells. A good example from antiquity is the hieroglyphs found on stones, monuments, or in caves in Egypt. Archaeologists have always without hesitation attributed those pictographs as coming from the hand of intelligent man, not some coincidence of wind and weather. Hieroglyphs thousands of years old are indisputably intelligently designed! This is true because they are not "natural" and convey information only an intelligent being could have designed on purpose. Modern information theory confirms this fact.

NASA was looking for a more sophisticated "signal" that would have required the application of modern information science to determine it was supernatural, i.e., not natural, and from the hand and mind of some intelligent extraterrestrial being out there somewhere. No such signal has ever been found, but maybe they were looking in the wrong places! The evidence of the intelligent design of life in the universe and, therefore, the existence of intelligent extraterrestrial beings was right below their noses ... literally.

In 1953 two scientists, Watson and Crick, discovered the double helix structure of the DNA molecule inside every living cell that seems to hold the key to differentiation of species, body plans, and cell types. Genes and chromosomes and their vital roles in the life of cells was already known. This was a huge biochemical breakthrough, but the most profound implications were not discovered until 1957 when Crick, a former code-breaker for the government during World War II, observed that the four letters, ATCG, which stand for the molecules which form the bridge between the spiral strands of sugar-phosphate were actually code, containing billions of possible combinations, only a select few of which would allow the DNA to instruct the production of functioning proteins appropriate to the organism to which belonged, which is DNA's purpose. (This is of course a highly simplified description.)

There it was—proof of intelligent design. Dr. Stephen Meyer calls it the "Signature in the Cell."

Science will never say something is impossible, they will say the probability of it is astronomically high, or low. What we can now say about DNA, is that the probability of it and other cellular structures forming in an undirected process in a prebiotic soup of sea water and various chemicals is astronomically low! Dr. James Tour, eminent synthetic organic chemist, points out that when it comes to forming complex organic molecules, even in a highly controlled laboratory setting, time is not on your side. That is, given enough time, all your work will decompose right back into smaller and simpler molecules. In the environmental remediation world where I spent several decades, we call that natural attenuation, large molecules degrade to smaller molecules over time. And this is not even talking about forming complex biomechanical structures as are found in cells.

Bottom line is that evidence of extraterrestrial intelligence has been found in living cells, and since we also now know the universe had a beginning it follows that the extraterrestrial intelligence must have its origin not in outer space, but outside space … and time. The alternative that space aliens, superior to ourselves, seeded our world with the code of life like themselves doesn't fly because that begs the question, where did they originate from? As per usual, however, I must admit, the majority of working scientists, especially evolutionary biologists (who have never made a complex molecule in their lives), are still on primordial soup and evolution of species bandwagons because their careers are based on it, even if it proves false one day … like the steady state universe did, pre-germ disease theory, nature of gravity, man-induced climate change, and many other "truths of science."

Information theory and science is now well developed, and it informs our thinking about the origins and nature of information. Whether a line of code in a computer program, a combination of blocks in a scrabble game, the sequence of letters in this document, or a chain of molecules in DNA, if it contains intelligible or functional information, it must have come from an intelligent mind, not a random or undirected process. What are the odds of dumping a box of scrabble chips on a board and every one lines up, right side up, to spell real words, and each one is perfectly positioned and aligned? Near zero, even if done a billion times over a billion years. This is not even approaching the astronomical odds against forming a DNA molecule that works by random mutation! But what would we conclude if we walked into a room to see a scrabble board all completed, every letter part of an intelligible word left to right and up and down, none spelled wrong, none upside down, no words right to left. This is what Crick found in DNA.

When I first read about the discovery of DNA coding in the 70s, I recognized that the digital information carrying capacity of DNA was akin to the machine-level computer code I'd been developing in the lab, and that functional code requires design, and design requires intelligence. If even one bit in a string of machine code was out of place, the instruction from the code to the machine became dysfunctional, so it could not be done by chance, no way. Simply stirring a pot of 1's and 0's and pouring them out in a line could not produce functional code, done a billion times, over a billion years. Functional code requires intelligent design, so does DNA and living cell structure.

Also, because of my physics background, I knew that the second law of thermodynamics applies even to biological systems ... entropy, order and all that stuff. Biologists have never even proposed a viable mechanism for emergence of the first multi-part living cell or the transformation of one species to another, either chemical or physical, and natural change through mutation or natural selection violated everything I knew about physics, including the math of the laws of probability and time. This was well before the electron microscope view of the cell was available, which now confirms my skepticism of "natural" biological evolution was justified.

Interesting stuff, but I had bigger fish to fry back then (circa 1985), so I put it aside for a future day when science would catch up and a theory of intelligent design could be formulated that did not rely on the Bible or the creation story, but strictly on science. That day has arrived. See YouTube for Steven Meyer or James Tour, if you'd like more details, including some amazing animations and actual electron microscope videos of a cell in operation, it's quite compelling.

So why does it matter? It matters because now we don't have to be bullied or intimidated by materialists, all of whom are leftists and atheists, who deny God's existence based on science or philosophy, introduced during the Enlightenment or Age of Reason in Marx and Darwin's day.

All the steady-staters are gone but it will take a few more decades for the God-is-dead crowd who believe in godless materialism to die off. Darwinian evolution is a pillar of their religion and they will hold on to tenaciously … their careers depend upon it!

Materialism is at the heart of Marxism and communism, but it's materialism, not God, which is dying in the twenty-first century!

CHAPTER 26
ⅢⱯⱤ𐐦ISⅢ VEⱤSUS ⱯⅢEⱤICⱯⒶISⅢ

Karl Marx, a mid-nineteenth century contemporary of Darwin's, though they never knew each other, glommed onto Darwin's concept and expanded his theory of socialism to become "social evolution" where the evolution from capitalism to communism was considered to be "inevitable," just a matter of time and circumstances. Marx also liked Darwin's theory because it supported his claim for "dialectical materialism" and denial of God, any god. They were both atheists and materialists.

Atheism is at the heart of Marx's communism. Without god, there is only inanimate matter operating undirected in a field of natural forces, like gravity, with no right or wrong. He called this dialectical materialism. Man is simply, according to Marx, the "graduate beast," at the top of the food chain, master of the realm, maker of his own destiny. Darwinism supports this view, much to Marx's delight. Man is, therefore, free to shape his world as he sees fit, without any constraints from, or allegiances to, a higher power than himself. Marx viewed this as a clean slate from which to develop his theories of socialism without regard to external constraints, like religion and traditional morality.

Why atheism and materialism matter?

Citizens and soldiers from the 40s and 50s in the U.S. and Canada who were turned by communists to betray their country all tell the same story. The first step in recruiting someone to communism is not a debate on Marxist theory of economic socialism, it is to have them join you in questioning the very existence of God and the meaning and purpose of life. Once they got God out of the way, it was relatively easy in that day, before we knew better, to convince an intelligent sophisticated person that the Soviet social justice system was superior to American capitalism which recently gave them the Great Depression ... and that the end justifies the means, including betraying one's own country, to create a better world for all.

This sounds familiar to the socialists' arguments today ... the evil capitalist pigs must be stopped, power to the people, down with greed, follow us, together we'll save the world. Eliminating God in this equation makes selling the idea of the salvation of man, by man, and for man a much easier and appealing proposition. This is why liberal democrat socialists like Pelosi, Omar, Sanders, Schumer, Biden, and their ilk want to remove God, especially Christianity from public life on the false premise of "separation of church and state" ... a phrase and concept not found in the Constitution. It is a goal of communism to marginalize or eliminate religion, not just from government and public life, but from the hearts and minds of the population, especially the youth. They do this by infiltration of Churches and the clergy, takeover of schools and teachers' organizations, rewriting textbooks, and leveraging front organizations like the ACLU to confound traditional American religious freedoms.

Remember the goals of communism for the destruction of America from the inside include:

- *Get control of the schools. Use them as transmission belts for socialism and current Communist propaganda. Soften the curriculum. Get control of teachers' associations. Put the party line in textbooks.*

- *Infiltrate the churches and replace revealed religion with "social" religion. Discredit the Bible and emphasize the need for intellectual maturity which does not need a "religious crutch."*

- *Eliminate prayer or any phase of religious expression in the schools on the grounds that it violates the principle of "separation of church and state."*

Now, juxtapose this godless materialistic worldview of Marx and his atheist comrades, including Darwin, with that of America's founders in the Declaration of Independence.

"We hold these truths to be self-evident, that all men are created equal, that they are endowed by their Creator with certain unalienable rights, that among these are Life, Liberty, and the pursuit of Happiness."

Both worldviews declare the inherent equality of men, but that's where the similarity ends. Marx's and Darwin's worldview is that our existence is a matter of chance and happenstance, to be made of it as you will. Jefferson's worldview describes men as having unalienable rights not granted by a monarch or a pope but endowed by the Creator Himself, implying we were created for some purpose … otherwise why the need for rights at all.

Christians, and most conservative Americans, believe we are part of an intelligent design, that we have both purpose for our own lives and obligations toward others' lives. We feel bound by both God's law and America's Constitution to live productive lives in service to God and country.

Marx and Darwin had no such constraints. Recruiting and training young converts in Marx/Darwin's world is much easier, and that is where many high school, college, and millennials find themselves today as the new-Marxism of democrat socialism sings its siren call to them 24/7, even in grade schools. Now you can see why the communist goal to "Take over schools, curriculum, teachers organization, textbooks, Hollywood, new media" is so important to them ... it prepares young gullible minds to receive the hard theories of socialism as the most moral and compassionate way to go, regardless of objective facts to the contrary. A person must be mentally preconditioned to prefer Marxist socialism over Jeffersonian capitalism.

Have your children or grandchildren been successfully recruited to democrat socialism, despite growing up in a loving Christian conservative home. Did you pay the recruiters (teachers and professors) to indoctrinate them and never bothered to investigate what they were being taught? Recent poll says 69 percent of high schoolers would vote for the socialist democrat candidate, only 23 percent for Trump. The numbers are similar for college and millennials. Unless we can turn this around, America is lost.

In 1776, after many years of debate, soul searching, thought, and prayer, a group of colonists decided to declare their independence from England and create a country of their own. They embraced the concept of a Creator God, religion, and morality as "self-evident" truths, necessary for a free people to prosper. Realizing that believers were at odds over specific doctrines the founding fathers forbade Congress to make any law respecting an establishment of religion, but they never contemplated freedom *from* religion as a general principle that could be consistent with "endowed by their Creator."

America's founding documents and principals depend entirely on the phrase, "...by their Creator." Without a Creator, America is no more than a materialistic, atheistic, Marxist/Darwinist state where anything goes ... survival of the fittest! Without a Creator, our rights are not "endowed," they are "allowed" ... by government, which is exactly what the founders wanted to avoid. Specific rights are enumerated in the first ten amendments, known as the Bill of Rights, but they all hinge on being endowed by God, not granted by government. And those rights not specifically enumerated to the federal government are to be retained by the people and the states.

The Constitution's main purpose was to protect the people from the government's natural tendency to get bigger and acquire more jurisdiction, power, and control over citizen's lives. Jefferson would turn over in his grave if he could see how far we have moved from those first principles of limited government he, Washington, Madison, Hamilton, Franklin, and others set out for the American experiment they called the United States of America, not the United Socialist Republics of America. Adams on the other hand argued for a strong central government.

Another label for liberals in the early twentieth century was progressives. This theory found easy acceptance among card carrying communists, communist sympathizers, liberal elites, academia, Hollywood, unions and other "useful idiots" in that day.

(From Hillsdale College's online course on the Constitution.)

> *"In the early 20th century, a new political theory— known as Progressivism—rose to prominence in America. This theory held that the principles of the American Founding, expressed most eloquently and concisely in the Declaration of Independence, were irrelevant to modern life. Progressives taught that stringent restrictions on government power were no longer necessary to protect liberty, since human nature and science had advanced greatly during the 19th century. Progressives did not believe that individuals are endowed with inalienable rights by a Creator; rather, they (like Marx) believed that rights are determined by social expediency and bestowed by the government. In conjunction with this new theory of rights, Progressivism holds that government must be able to adapt to ever-changing historical circumstances."*

Progressivism became synonymous with liberalism in the latter half of the twentieth century. Liberal federal district judges and Supreme Court Justices proceeded to legislate from the bench and felt no qualms about doing so. The Constitution was not only liberally interpreted it was ignored in deference to their enlightened worldview, which was perhaps unintentionally, but consequentially, simpatico with the Soviet communists forty-five goals for the destruction of America from the inside! Go figure.

How would you like to find out your worldview is "having or characterized by shared attributes or interests, i.e., compatible" with Soviet communists' goals for America's destruction? If you are a democrat in 2020, this is your reality.

The era of judicial activism gave us Roe v. Wade, removing prayer from schools, and many other nontraditional American values rulings. To describe judges as activist in this sense is to argue that they decide cases on the basis of their own policy preferences rather than a faithful interpretation of the law, thus abandoning the impartial judicial role and "legislating from the bench." Decisions may be labeled activist either for striking down legislative or executive action or for allowing it to stand.

Liberal democrats and their comrades were winning the war against our Constitution, but then along came the man they didn't count on … and just like that, the Constitution is restored.

Not all democrats are liberal activists or progressives, but all liberal activists and progressives are democrats or worse, Marxists!

The main purpose of Marxism is to dissolve society into a classless, stateless, egalitarian system where only the ruling elite make decisions for the masses, for their own good, of course. American capitalism and Marxist socialism are completely incompatible and have irreconcilable differences, the most foundational of which is: our rights are endowed by our Creator, not allowed by our government.

Jefferson was a man of the Enlightenment, the Age of Reason, and did not believe in miracles. But he knew that if America was to survive it would only be among a moral and religious people. Jefferson attend church services regularly, held in the halls of Congress! "Our **constitution** was made only for a **moral** and religious **people**," **said** President John Adams. Our country depends on the mores of its citizens, and "Where mores are sufficient, laws are unnecessary; where mores are insufficient, laws are unenforceable." Consider the uncontrollable riots of 1968, Watts, Rodney King, Ferguson, and Berkeley. And now in 2020, the riots, lootings, arson, and anarchy going on across the country's democrat-controlled states and cities.

Karl Marx and Charles Darwin, contemporaries in the mid-nineteenth century postulated theories of both social and natural evolution which would have profound implications for all of mankind for the foreseeable future ... none of them good! But the good news is that modern science, both social, political, and physical, will hopefully render them all to the ashbin of history within the next decades of so. In the meantime, their influence continues to cause disruption and chaos for tens of millions of citizens of the world, and unless we defeat them at the ballot box in 2020, many bad things will happen.

CHAPTER 27
FROM THE COMMUNIST MANIFESTO TO DEMOCRATIC SOCIALISM

In 1848, two young educated men named Karl Marx and Friedrich Engels, both devout materialists, published a pamphlet called *The Communist Manifesto*. They did not invent communism or create the unrest among the populace at the time. In Europe, the Communist League of working men was already established and the living and working conditions of all but the nobility, the clergy, and the wealthy capitalists of the mid 1800s was horrendous. Even in America, life was tough if you were not a landowner, were a slave, or just a working stiff. These were the horse and buggy days of dark nights, freezing cold, sweltering heat, and swarming pests ... not the good old days! Conditions for revolution were ripe.

The pampered snowflakes of today's left know nothing of real poverty, hopelessness, racism, pollution, and social injustice. Saul Alinsky would find a way to get to the pampered middle-class youth over a hundred years later, but that's another story.

What Marx did was codify "communism," i.e., give the movement structure, doctrine, justification, and a game plan ... much as Saul Alinsky did over a hundred years later in 1971 with his book *Rules for Radicals*.

Notice in these next sections the frequent use of the word social, society, socialism, which are underlined for emphasis. Communism is at its foundation obsessed with changing society, a collective of individuals, from what it is to what they believe it should be…a collectivist socialist partocracy. Marx, a devout atheist, believed it was not individual people who created injustice, poverty and tyranny, it was society and its institutions and if both these could just be organized properly a rationale utopia of social justice could be achieved; each individual working according to his ability and paid according to his need…the rewards of the most productive spread around among the least productive, by force if necessary. Communist/Socialist states are always set up to control the people and force conformance with the dictates of the party. America's founders, on the other hand, believed in the private life, liberty, property, and pursuit of happiness of the individual; each working to the best of his ability and paid according to the value each person produced, with no expectation of equal outcomes or equal happiness. The American Constitution set up a framework for living together in maximum individual freedom while constraining the government from taking away a person's property, possessions, life, liberty, and pursuit of happiness. Communists, Socialists, Liberals, Progressives, and Democrat Socialists are all basically Marxists in political philosophy. Democrats were the party of slavery, lynching's, Jim Crow, and the KKK; now they are the party of socialism, abortion, Obama/Biden, Black Lives Matter and Antifa. No patriotic, religious, law-abiding, pro-life American should vote for such people?

The Communist Manifesto – Karl Marx, Friedrich Engels, 1848

> *"The Communist Manifesto, originally the Manifesto of the Communist Party is an 1848 political pamphlet by the German philosophers Karl Marx and Friedrich Engels. Commissioned by the Communist League and originally published in London just as the Revolutions of 1848 began to erupt, the Manifesto was later recognized as one of the world's most influential political documents. It presents an analytical approach to the class struggle (historical and then-present) and the conflicts of*

capitalism and the capitalist mode of production, rather than a prediction of communism's potential future forms. The Communist Manifesto summarizes Marx and Engels' theories concerning the nature of society and politics, namely that in their own words 'the history of all hitherto existing society is the history of class struggles'. It also briefly features their ideas for how the capitalist society of the time would eventually be replaced by socialism. In the last paragraph of the Manifesto, the authors call for a 'forcible overthrow of all existing social conditions', which served as the justification for all communist revolutions around the world."

Marx and Engels went on to write scholarly technical works on the subject of capital production and distribution, *Das Kapital*, Vol 1 by Marx, Vol 2–3 by Engels, based on notes from Marx who was by that time deceased, and no longer an atheist. Some said they were so detailed and tedious in theory nobody, not even the communists, read them. It is said Marx sent Darwin a copy of *Das Kapital*, which Darwin thanked him for but never read.

The Wikipedia description of the *Communist Manifesto* above is excellent and pretty much says it all.

I repeat the last sentences here for emphasis and relevance to our day when the forces of socialism are trying so hard to repeal and replace America with a socialist-style government. (Emphasis added.)

"The history of all hitherto existing society is the history of class struggles." It also briefly features their ideas for how the capitalist society of the time would eventually be replaced by socialism. In the last paragraph of the Manifesto, the authors call for a 'forcible overthrow of all existing social conditions', which served as the justification for all communist revolutions around the world."

Class Struggles, capitalism replaced by socialism, forcible overthrow of all existing social conditions. The riots of 2020 are not about the horrible injustice of George Floyd's death by a Minneapolis Police office, that's just the most recent excuse for anarchy. These riots, like those from decades ago are about revolution not reformation. They are instigated, organized, and paid for by people like George Soros and his ilk, using Black Lives Matter, Antifa, and other anti-white, anti-government hate groups, and disgruntled brainwashed liberal young people, blacks and whites, to do their dirty work. And while they riot, loot, burn, and occupy the silent majority of patriotic law-abiding American's who are not racist or suffer from white guilt are seething in anger and disdain for what is being done to our country, enabled by democrat governors and mayors. Not happening in Republican controlled areas. Let that sink in for a minute…and vote wisely in November. Marxism, later called communism, interchangeable with socialism, is undeniably the root of the modern democrat socialist ideology. Other ideologies which were spawned from Marxism include fascism and Nazism, fierce competitors but close cousins. My point here is to expose the common heritage for all these disruptive socialist ideologies and their ideological link to modern democratic socialism.

Dinesh D'Souza makes a strong case that all these are left-wing, not right-wing ideologies … all resulting in state control of nearly every aspect of a person's life. The proponents of communism, fascism, Nazism, and democratic socialism all want the same thing: "to change society from what it is to what they believe it should be!" This is a close quote from Saul Alinsky's book *Rules for Radicals* in 1971.

Here is a description of what democratic socialists ultimately want, since their ideological heritage is Marxist in orientation. The following was prepared from a compilation of quote fragments from the detailed descriptions that follow:

Democrat socialists desire *a socioeconomic order structured upon the ideas of common ownership of the means
of production and the absence of social classes, money,
and the state, ultimately to be resolved through a social
revolution. This revolution will put the working class in
power, aimed to overcome social divisions and create a
homogeneous society by convincing all parts of the new
socialist society to subordinate their personal interests to
the "common good," accepting political interests as the
main priority of economic organization, with an emphasis on workers' self-management and democratic control
of economic institutions within a market or some form
of a decentralized planned socialist economy. Democratic
socialists argue that American capitalism is inherently
incompatible with the values of freedom, equality, and
solidarity and that these ideals can be achieved only
through the realization of a socialist society. It rejects
assertions that violence is automatically negative in
nature and views political violence as means that can
achieve national rejuvenation.* —Wikipedia compilation

Religious, law-abiding, self-reliant, conservatives argue that democratic socialism is inherently incompatible with traditional American
values of life, liberty, property, and the pursuit of happiness in a constitutional, free-enterprise, entrepreneurial society.

Obama, Clinton, Biden, Sanders, Warren, Pelosi, Schumer,
Schiff, Nadler, AOC, and Omar are all democratic socialists, or worse.

Modern democratic socialism is the anti-American political
evolution of communism, fascism, Nazism, and socialism … all having their roots in *The Communist Manifesto* of Karl Marx.

Communism

*Communism is a philosophical, social, political, and eco-
nomic ideology and movement whose ultimate goal is the*

establishment of a communist society, which is a socioeconomic order structured upon the ideas of common ownership of the means of production and the absence of social classes, money, and the state.

Communism includes a variety of schools of thought. All of these share the analysis that the current order of society stems from its economic system, capitalism; that in this system there are two major social classes; that conflict between these two classes is the root of all problems in society; and that this situation will ultimately be resolved through a social revolution. The two classes are the working class—who must work to survive and who make up the majority within society—and the capitalist class—a minority who derives profit from employing the working class through private ownership of the means of production. The revolution will put the working class in power and in turn establish social ownership of the means of production, which according to this analysis is the primary element in the transformation of society toward communism.

Fascism

Fascists believe that liberal democracy is obsolete and regard the complete mobilization of society under a totalitarian one-party state as necessary to prepare a nation for armed conflict and to respond effectively to economic difficulties. Such a state is led by a strong leader—such as a dictator and a martial government composed of the members of the governing fascist party—to forge national unity and maintain a stable and orderly society. Fascism rejects assertions that violence is automatically negative in nature and views political violence, war, and imperialism as means that can achieve national rejuvenation.

Fascists advocate a mixed economy, with the principal goal of achieving autarky (national economic self-sufficiency) through protectionist and interventionist economic policies.

Nazism

Officially the National Socialist German Workers' Party, Nazism subscribed to pseudo-scientific theories of racial hierarchy and social Darwinism, identifying the Germans as a part of what the Nazis regarded as an Aryan or Nordic master race. It aimed to overcome social divisions and create a German homogeneous society based on racial purity which represented a people's community. The term "National Socialism" arose out of attempts to create a nationalist redefinition of "socialism," as an alternative to both Marxist international socialism and free market capitalism. Nazism rejected the Marxist concepts of class conflict and universal equality, opposed cosmopolitan internationalism, and sought to convince all parts of the new German society to subordinate their personal interests to the "common good," accepting political interests as the main priority of economic organization.

Socialism

The socialist political movement includes a set of political philosophies that originated in the revolutionary movements of the mid-to-late eighteenth century and out of concern for the social problems that were associated with capitalism. By the late nineteenth century, after the work of Karl Marx and his collaborator Friedrich Engels, socialism had come to signify opposition to capitalism and advocacy for a post-capitalist system based on some form of social ownership of the means of production.

By the 1920s, social democracy and communism had become the two dominant political tendencies within the international socialist movement. By this time, socialism emerged as "the most influential secular movement of the twentieth century, worldwide."

Author's note: in the 20s and 30s, many American elites and intellectuals bought into secular socialism, and even into Soviet socialism. Some were recruited by Moscow and went on to become spies for Russia and traitors to their country, as documented elsewhere in this book.

Democratic Socialism

Democratic socialism is a socialist political philosophy which advocates political democracy alongside a socially owned economy, with an emphasis on workers' self-management and democratic control of economic institutions within a market or some form of a decentralized planned socialist economy. Democratic socialists argue that capitalism is inherently incompatible with the values of freedom, equality and solidarity and that these ideals can be achieved only through the realization of a socialist society. Although most democratic socialists are seeking a very gradual transition to socialism, democratic socialism can support either revolutionary or reformist politics as a means to establish socialism ... democratic socialism is distinguished on the basis that democratic socialists are committed to systemic transformation of the economy from capitalism to socialism.

In contrast to modern social democrats, democratic socialists believe that policy reforms and state interventions aimed at addressing social inequalities and suppressing the economic contradictions of capitalism will ultimately exacerbate the contradictions, seeing them emerge elsewhere in the economy under a different guise. Democratic socialists believe the fundamental issues with capitalism are systemic in nature and can only be resolved by replacing the capitalist economic system with social-ism, i.e., by (repealing and) *replacing private ownership with collective ownership of the means of production and extending democracy to the economic sphere.*

If much of this sounds familiar, it is! It's the underlying ideology of the modern national democrat party, who are running socialist candidates for president and Congress. It is also the underlying ideology of most university professors and administrators who are not shy about force feeding their impressionable students with their beliefs.

CHAPTER 28
THE NAKED COMMUNIST—COMMUNISM EXPOSED

In the 1920s, Marxist socialism intrigued many American intellectuals and elites. After the stock market crash of 1929 and the following deep depression, it was easier for communist recruiters to entice a disgruntled generation of Americans to reject capitalism and representative democracy, which had failed them, and try a different way ... socialism and Soviet-style partocracy. Roosevelt himself was actually an admirer of many of the tenants of Soviet communism, and even Mussolini's fascism. Some historians and observers say the New Deal, Social Security, and other Rooseveltian programs were socialistic. I say Roosevelt did everything and anything he could to keep poor jobless Americans from starving in poverty ... whatever you want to call it. Desperate times call for desperate measures. The Great Depression lasted from 1929–1942. The Soviets took advantage of that time to infiltrate the Roosevelt administration, Hollywood, the news media, the Church, the schools, and universities. Many Americans on the left coast, Chicago, NYC, DC, Columbia, and Harvard Universities fashionably became communist "sympathizers." Some, like Alger Hiss, Whitaker Chambers, and others betrayed their country to become Soviet spies with direction and support from Moscow.

J. Edgar Hoover, director of the newly formed FBI paid attention, and would later take down most of the Soviet's spy rings, with the help of a repentant Chambers. Chambers' full story is told in his book, Witness … an interesting read. Chambers was recruited using the old "God doesn't exist" pitch communists always lead with. While at Columbia, Obama's alma mater, a young Chambers was brainwashed and prepared for communism's appeal. In his book *The Witness and the President*, K. Alan Snyder explains, "Columbia, in its quest to create a nihilist, had instead created a communist." More on Chamber's story in a following chapter. While a Soviet communist spy who had rejected religion and god, Chambers had an epiphany when feeding his young daughter. Observing the beautiful complexity of her eyes and face Chambers reasoned there must be a God because nothing that complex could possibly come into being without a grand design, and a grand designer. Karl Marx and Charles Darwin would beg to differ. This caused him to begin to question the entire premise of communism and to reassess the claims of the Bible and religion he had previously rejected. Several years later he committed his life to Christ, left the CP, and joined a Quaker church.

Authors note: Communism relies on dialectical materialism, which is inherently atheistic. It is logically impossible to be both a Christian and a communist. It is also not possible to enjoy the unalienable rights of life, liberty, and the pursuit of happiness without a Creator God who endowed us with them, per America's Declaration of Independence. Communist recruiters always lead with the "God is a myth" argument. So, what do liberal recruiters, like university professors, lead with? Whittaker Chambers became a liberal nihilist while at Columbia, a hotbed of Marxist advocacy. A young Barack Obama would receive the same indoctrination decades later, but he would follow Saul Alinsky's "community organizer" model of socialism rather that Soviet communism. Once Chamber's mind was prepared by the pro-Soviet liberal professors at Columbia, it was only a short hop to Marxist communism … from having nothing to believe in to having something he'd be willing to die for.

> *"Nihilism is a viewpoint that traditional values and beliefs are unfounded and that existence is senseless and useless; a doctrine that denies any objective ground of truth and especially of moral truths; a doctrine or belief that conditions in the social organization are so bad as to make destruction desirable for its own sake independent of any constructive program or possibility." —Merriam-Webster*

Karl Marx was an archetypical nihilist and so are many liberal professors teaching our children and grandchildren in colleges and universities across America today. How else can we explain sending them to school from patriotic, conservative, pro-life, Christian conservative homes and having them return anti-American, cynical, pro-abortion, irreligious, liberal socialists. Most of us were young and stupid at that age, but only indoctrination can make a nihilist, a socialist, or a communist. This also explains why Bernie Sanders, a communist sympathizer and committed socialist has such a huge youth following. The reader should be aware that Karl Marx started all this, V.I. Lenin, Joseph Stalin, and their successors in the Soviet Union perpetuated it, and American elites and bohemians in movies, TV, entertainment, academia, news and magazines, government, business, law, religion, and politics (democrats) brought it home as "liberalism," like Reagan warned: "If Communism ever comes to America, it will come in the form of Liberalism."

Most readers are aware that Soviet Russia under Joseph Stalin joined America and its allies to defeat Nazi Germany but that was a self-serving move and Stalin kept up Soviet espionage all through the war. He even had a spy inside the Manhattan Project that developed the atomic bomb. After World War II, it was back to business as usual for the ambitious Soviet communists. Their goal was world domination, but they would have to deal with the United States to achieve that goal.

An FBI agent named W. Cleon Skousen, a friend, associate, and respected confident of J. Edgar Hoover, wrote a book in 1958 which would become the textbook for the FBI, CIA, and others trying to understand communism, especially Soviet communism. Since it laid bare the tenants of communism someone suggested he title the book *The Naked Communist.*

What follows is what we need to know in 2020 about the Soviet communist goals which they believed would lead to the destruction of America, from the inside. You may be shocked that all but one of the forty-five goals have been achieved and are still wreaking havoc in America society today. This is relevant in 2020 because, as you will see, all these goals are liberal democrat socialist goals, not conservative republican capitalist goals!

At Mr. Roddam's (Hillary's dad) funeral, Bill gave the eulogy. He thought he was being cute by recounting Mr. Roddam's first reaction to Hillary agreeing to marry him. "He thought that being a democrat was about the next thing to being a communist." Mr. Roddam must have read *the Naked Communist* too!

The forty-five goals of communism were read into the Congressional Record by Albert S. Herlong, Jr (D-Florida) in 1963, the same year JFK was assassinated, probably by communists and their gangster allies in Cuba and America.

By 1962, the communists of the Soviet Union had a solid base of spies and sympathizers in the United States, in government, academia, Hollywood, the news media, churches, and unions ... as described elsewhere in this book. They had been working their plan of subversion for decades, but in the late 50s the House Un-American Activities Committee (HUAC), Senator Joe McCarthy, and J. Edgar Hoover had stalled their progress. After pounding his shoe on the podium at the UN and screaming, "We will bury you" at the U.S., an impatient Nikita Khrushchev almost overplayed his hand, and President JFK forced him to withdraw Soviet nuclear missiles from

Cuba, just 90 miles of our coast. I remember the Cuban Missile Crisis well.

Communism/socialism and communists/socialists were bad words back then. Who could have predicted that sixty years later a majority of young Americans and millions of adults would prefer big-government socialism over free-enterprise capitalism? That this a fact of life in 2020 is evidence of the success of the "forty-five goals." You will recognize, as I did in 1975, these goals, originally developed by Soviet communists to destroy America from within, are leftist by nature and many of them have long been democrat party initiatives and positions. Skousen, the Russians, nor anyone in Washington could have contemplated the coming of Ronald Reagan in the 80s and the subsequent fall of the Soviet Empire in the 90s. The Evil Empire fell but Russia, China, North Korea, Cuba, Venezuela, and a host of other communist countries survived, as did their destructive tyrannical ideology, communism/socialism.

The United States is now the most powerful country in the world and could make any nation—communist, Islamist, whatever—pay a price they would not be willing to pay in a full-scale war but that is not our present threat. Like Rome, our greatest threat is from within, from the infection of our youth, politicians, academics, media, entertainment, churches, unions, and businesses with a communist/socialist ideology which harkens back to the old Soviet Union and Karl Marx before that. The Democratic Socialist Party of 2020 is now the standard bearer of this political ideology.

No one in the Democratic party or their allies in the media, certainly not in Washington, could have imagined the coming of Donald J. Trump in 2016, and like Reagan, when he gets reelected to a second term, he is going to unwind their progressive policies and build fortresses against their return for a generation, e.g., conservative federal judges, Supreme Court Justices, border walls, dismantled regulations, empowered military, strong economy, etc.

As you read these communist goals below, remember who wrote them, not me, and to put them in context of the times in which they were developed. Some are archaic, some may be offensive to us today, some may seem laughable, but I think you will see why reading these, as I did in 1975, help to connect the dots for me regarding where the liberal democrats of that day, not the party of JFK anymore, but of LBJ, George McGovern, Saul Alinsky, and sixties' radicals, may have gotten their ideas.

I found it disconcerting to read something so detailed and consistently well organized and purposeful, gleaned from the United States' mortal enemy, the communist Soviet Union, could be so aligned with the "liberal" ideology generally, and the Democratic Party specifically. It was shocking to be honest and it took me years of additional study and observations to accept what was obvious on its face ... the Democratic Party had been "captured" by communists, see goal #15 below.

I'm not saying Johnson, or any other specific politician, was a communist, but I found it more than coincidental the lurch to the left by the then Democratic Party and its associated allies in the media, teacher's union, academia, churches, and other traditionally conservative institutions was seemingly the result of some scheme hatched by Soviet communists decades earlier. I was not a republican in those days ... heck I wasn't anything, just beginning a career, raising a family, teaching youth Sunday School, playing some golf, partying every weekend, minding my own business.

Could it really be that the Democratic Party and vital American institutions had been co-opted by those who held goals for the destruction of America? And if so, why on earth would they want to do that? This also fit the pattern I observed by charting the votes of democrats and republicans on issues of interest to my company, a major steel producer. Over a two-year period, democrats across twelve states voted against my interest and for the union interest, 95 percent of the time, republicans just the opposite ... another data point, and as a scientist (applied physics), I'm all about data.

Then I read Saul Alinsky's *Rules for Radicals* (1971), described elsewhere in this book, and it all gelled. I came to believe then, and still do now, the liberal/progressive/leftist/socialist agendas we see playing out in so many ways today are not random collections of ideas from patriotic American individuals with different views and opinions, although it may seem that way. There is a pattern here, a method to their madness, a plan for their progress ... and it all traces back to the socialism of Karl Marx and the communism of V.I. Lenin, specifically enumerated, more or less, in the forty-five goals described in Skousen's book.

I sincerely believe the same people who pursued these goals for the destruction of America in the past are the ones who assassinated JFK in 1963. Lee Harvey Oswald *may* have pulled the trigger, but he was not alone in wanting JFK, and later his brother Bobby, and Dr. M.L. King eliminated. The following regime of Lyndon Johnson would usher in the modern welfare state, micro-mismanaging the Vietnam war, and a host of other policies that must have made the commies in the Kremlin, Beijing, Washington, Chicago, NYC, and the left coast smile.

After Nixon bombed North Vietnam into allowing us to surrender, the sympathizers in the congress (democrats) pulled all support from the South Vietnamese resulting in the slaughter of over 2 million Vietnamese, Cambodians, and Laotians. Commies around the world, John Kerry and Jane Fonda, celebrated our defeat and the communist victory.

The World War II war hero turned ultra-liberal, George McGovern became the standard-bearer of the political left which reached its ideological zenith under his leadership and influence. But he also split the party and when he lost resoundingly to Richard Nixon in 1972, the party reassessed its overreach, not its ideology, and took a visible turn toward centrist directions, e.g. Jimmy

Carter, Bill Clinton. McGovern said, "We made a serious effort to open the doors of the Democratic Party (to liberals and activists of all stripes)—and as soon as we did, half the democrats walked out." I believe that is what we are seeing with the Trump revolution … patriotic democrats are walking away from the Democratic Socialist Party of Sanders, Biden, Pelosi, Warren, Schumer … like Ronald Reagan and many others did in the past.

CHAPTER 29
THE FORTY-FIVE COMMUNIST GOALS FOR DESTRUCTION OF AMERICA

So, here are the forty-five goals. I highlighted those that jumped out at me in 1975, and still do! Keep in mind these were developed decades ago by Soviet communists who sought the destruction of America and they believed these goals provided a road map. They are so straight forward and succinct; no further comment is required by me here. If you are interested, buy the book *The Naked Communist*, by W. Cleon Skousen, get the newest edition 2017.

> "You will be alarmed, you will be informed, and you'll be glad you read W. Cleon Skousen" —Ronald Reagan

> "*The Naked Communist* lays out the whole progressive agenda." —Dr. Ben Carson

1. U.S. acceptance of coexistence as the only alternative to atomic war.

2. U.S. willingness to capitulate in preference to atomic war.

3. Develop the illusion that total disarmament by the United States would be a demonstration of moral strength.

4. Permit free trade between nations regardless of communist affiliation and regardless of whether or not items could be used for war.

5. Extension of long-term loans to Russia and Soviet Satellites.

6. Provide American aid to all nations regardless of Communist domination.

7. *Grant recognition of Red China. Admission of Red China to the U.N.*

8. Set up East and West Germany as separate states in spite of Khrushchev's promise in 1955 to settle the Germany question by free elections under supervision of the U.N.

9. Prolong the conferences to ban atomic tests because the U.S. has agreed to suspend tests as long as negotiations are in progress.

10. Allow all Soviet Satellites individual representation in the U.N.

11. *Promote the U.N. as the only hope for mankind. If its charter is rewritten, demand that it is set up as one-world government with its own independent armed forces.*

12. *Resist any attempt to outlaw the Communist Party.*

13. *Do away with all loyalty oaths.*

14. Continue giving Russia access to the U.S. Patent Office.

15. *Capture one or both political parties in the United States.*

16. *Use technical decisions of the courts to weaken basic American institutions by claiming their activities violate rights.*

17. *Get control of the schools. Use them as transmission belts for socialism and current Communist propaganda. Soften the curriculum. Get control of teachers' associations. Put the party line in textbooks.*

18. *Gain control of all student newspapers.*

19. *Use student riots to foment public protests against programs or organizations which are under Communist attack.*

20. *Infiltrate the press. Get control of book-review assignments, editorial writing, and policy-making positions.*

21. *Gain control of key positions in radio, TV and pictures.*

22. *Continue discrediting American culture by degrading all forms of artistic expression. An American Communist cell was told to "eliminate all good sculpture from parks and building, substitute shapeless, awkward and meaningless forms."*

23. *Control art critics and directors of art museums. "Our plan it to promote ugliness, repulsive meaningless art."*

24. *Eliminate all laws governing obscenity by calling them "censorship" and a violation of free speech and free press.*

25. *Breakdown cultural standard of morality by promoting pornography and obscenity in books, magazines, motion pictures, radio and TV.*

26. *Present homosexuality, degeneracy and promiscuity as "normal, natural, and healthy."*

27. *Infiltrate the churches and replace revealed religion with "social" religion. Discredit the Bible and emphasize the need for intellectual maturity which does not need a "religious crutch."*

28. *Eliminate prayer or any phase of religious expression in the schools on the grounds that it violates the principle of "separation of church and state."*

29. *Discredit the American Constitution by calling it inadequate, old-fashioned, out of step with modern needs, a hindrance to cooperation between nations on a world-wide basis.*

30. *Discredit the American founding fathers. Present them as selfish aristocrats who had no concern for the "common man."*

31. *Belittle all forms of American culture and discourage the teaching of American history on the ground that it was only a minor part of "the big picture." Give more emphasis to Russian history since the Communists took over.*

32. *Support any socialist movement to give centralized control over any part of the culture—education, social agencies, welfare programs, mental health clinics, etc.*

33. *Eliminate all laws or procedures which interfere with the operation of the Communist apparatus.*

34. *Eliminate the House Committee on Un-American Activities (HUAC).*

35. *Discredit and eventually dismantle the FBI.*

36. *Infiltrate and gain control of more unions.*

37. *Infiltrate and gain control of big business.*

38. *Transfer some of the powers of arrest from the police to social agencies. Treat all behavioral problems as psychiatric disorders which no one but psychiatrists can understand or treat.*

39. *Dominate the psychiatric profession and use mental health laws as a means of gaining coercive control over those who oppose Communist goals.*

40. *Discredit the family as an institution. Encourage promiscuity and easy divorce.*

41. *Emphasize the need to raise children away from the negative influence of parents. Attribute prejudices, mental blocks and retarding of children to suppressive influence of parents.*

42. *Create the impression that violence and insurrection are legitimate aspects of the American tradition; that students and special-interest groups should rise up and use "united force" to solve economic, political or social problems.*

43. *Overthrow all colonial governments before naïve populations are ready for self-government.*

44. *Internationalize the Panama Canal*

45. Repeal the Connally Reservation so the U.S. cannot prevent the World Court from seizing jurisdiction over domestic problems. Give the World Court jurisdiction over nations and individuals alike.

It can be no coincidence that the "Liberal Agenda" democrats have pursued over the last seventy-five years or so got many of its marching orders from this list. That they have so clearly pursued goals of

Soviet communism for the destruction of America is their treasonous sin. That they are now using illegal and clandestine means toward those ends is their prosecutable crime. This book indicts them; you, the voter, must convict them in November.

CHAPTER 30
THE STRANGE CASE OF WHITTAKER CHAMBERS AND ALGER HISS

No book about communism's influence on American politics would be complete without a chapter about the most influential person you probably never heard of—Whittaker Chambers. Ronald Reagan quoted his book *Witness* often in speeches and letters. This autobiography of Chambers was a *New York Times* Best Seller for thirteen weeks in a row in 1952. It was the influence of Chambers, more than any other person, that made Reagan into the fierce commie fighter that he became, first in Hollywood, then in the Whitehouse.

> "Whittaker Chambers, born Jay Vivian Chambers (April 1, 1901–July 9, 1961), was an American writer-editor and former Communist spy who in 1948 testified about Communist espionage, thereafter, earning respect from the American Conservative movement (*especially arch conservative William F. Buckley who founded National Review magazine in 1955*). After early years as a Communist Party member (1925) and Soviet spy (1932–1938), he defected from the Soviet underground (1938) and joined *Time* magazine (1939–1948). Under subpoena in 1948, he testified about the Ware group in what became the Hiss case for perjury (1949–1950), all described in his 1952 memoir *Witness*. Afterwards,

he worked briefly as a senior editor at *National Review* (1957–1959). President Ronald Reagan awarded him the Presidential Medal of Freedom posthumously in 1984."

"The Ware Group was a covert organization of Communist Party USA operatives within the United States government in the 1930s, run first by Harold Ware (1889–1935) and then by Whittaker Chambers after Ware's accidental death on August 13, 1935.

Harold Ware founded this group under the auspices of J. Peters by Summer 1933. Ware was a CP official working for the federal government in Washington, D.C.

His main lifelong interest was agriculture but his mother said, "His interest in economics and politics developed intensely at this time, and while at college he wrote me constantly for the latest news of the socialist movement," first a socialist, then a communist! He was typical of young intellectuals of his day.

The first known meeting of the Ware Group occurred in late 1933 with eight members: John Abt, Henry Collins, Alger Hiss, Victor Perlo, Lee Pressman, Nathaniel Weyl, and Nathan Witt.

Initially, Peters instructed that members make "exceptional money sacrifices" to the Party, study Marxist theory and Party doctrine, observe "strictest secrecy," and to obtain "any government documents" available to them.

By 1934, the group had grown to some seventy-five members, divided into cells. Members initially joined Marxist study groups and then into activities on behalf of the party. They shared a belief that Marxist ideologies were the correct way to approach the problems of the ongoing Great Depression (*which began in October 1929*). Chambers also stated that Ware could have been acting "pursuant to orders from the Central Committee of the Communist Party of the United States."

The Ware group started among young lawyers and economists hired by the Agricultural Adjustment Administration (AAA). This New Deal agency reported to the Secretary of Agriculture but was operated independently of Department of Agriculture bureaucracy. All the members of the Ware Group were dues paying members of the CP. *This was not illegal or considered subversive in the 30s, in fact being a communist or at least a communist sympathizer was fashionable among elites, intellectuals, actors, academics, and urban bohemians back then. Progressing to the "underground," passing government documents to the American Communist Party, then to Moscow, was espionage and highly illegal.*

Members of the group joined other "apparatuses" under Chambers.

The group may have folded as such upon Chambers' defection from the Soviet underground in 1938. Some members seemed to have joined other groups, as attested by Elizabeth Bentley (*Columbia U graduate*), including Victor Perlo and George Silverman.

"Alger Hiss (November 11, 1904–November 15, 1996, *Johns Hopkins Phi Beta Kappa, then Harvard Law*) was an American government official who was accused of spying for the Soviet Union in 1948, but statutes of limitations had expired for espionage. He was convicted of perjury in connection with this charge in 1950. Before the trial he was involved in the establishment of the United Nations both as a U.S. State Department official and as a U.N. official. In later life, he worked as a lecturer and author.

Hiss was a brilliant student and lawyer, impressive in speech and statue, and the darling of liberal elites on both coasts. In those days, the only difference between a liberal and communist was one carried a card and the other didn't. It was not illegal to be a communist party member, but espionage was, still the case today.

Definition: Espionage or spying is the act of obtaining secret or confidential information or divulging of the same without the permission of the holder of the information. Spies help agencies uncover secret information. Any individual or spy ring (a cooperating group of spies), in the service of a government, company or independent operation, can commit espionage. The practice is clandestine, as it is unwelcome. In some circumstances it may be a legal tool of law enforcement and in others it may be illegal. Spying is what Obama Justice Department and FBI did to the Trump campaign in 2016 and 2017.

> *What Chambers, Ware, Hiss, and their comrades were doing was definitely illegal ... also immoral, disloyal, and potentially treasonous ... but not to liberals and communists where the end always justifies the means. Since they owe no allegiance to God, anything goes ... Man is his own God, just like Karl Marx said. Chambers had immunity from prosecution for his testimony; Hiss did not and lied with conviction, making things up, telling tales, denying facts and testimony in spite of evidence to the contrary, accusing Chambers of mental illness ... you know, like Adam Schiff did prosecuting Trump in his impeachment investigation. Liberals in the press, wall street, the government, and academia applauded Hiss and disparaged Chambers ... sound familiar? Of Schiff, Oklahoma Senator James Imhoff said he had never seen anyone lie with such conviction. Hiss looking up from hell would be proud of Schiff.*

On August 3, 1948, Whittaker Chambers, a former U.S. CP member, testified under subpoena before the HUAC that Hiss had secretly been a communist while in federal service. Hiss categorically denied the charge. During the pretrial discovery process, Chambers produced new evidence, documents he hid years before and some microfilm hidden inside a pumpkin, indicating that he and Hiss had been involved in espionage. A federal grand jury indicted Hiss on two counts of perjury. After a mistrial due to a hung jury, Hiss was tried a second time, and, in January 1950, he was found guilty and received two concurrent five-year sentences, of which he eventually served three and a half years." —Wikipedia composite (Emphasis added.)

So ... justice was no more served back then that it is today. Liberals, leftist, socialists, communists, and Roosevelt democrats mostly got away with everything they did back then, and still do today ... being aggregated into one unity party, the Democratic Socialist Party of LBJ, Carter, Clinton, Obama, Biden, Hillary, Warren, AOC, Omar, Pelosi, Schumer ... and last but certainly not least, George Soros.

Liberals in that day not only defended their favorite liberal and communist, Hiss, but viciously attacked and smeared Chambers, like they do Clinton and Trump today. Hiss vigorously denied all the accusations, like Clinton, for years but after many authors investigating the matter, new evidence, de-classification of secret documents, and testimony from others of the Ware Group, the overwhelming evidence and legal opinion of most investigators since that time are that Hiss was the lying communist spy Chambers said he was. Schiff is a lying, liberal, leaking, loser and crooked Hillary is guilty as sin, but both are free as a bird! Hopefully, the John Durham legal investigations will produce some prosecutions, but I'm not holding my breath. democrats, mostly lawyer themselves, seem to know how to play the game, push the limits, never get caught without plausible deniability better than republicans ... go figure!

So, what did Hiss actually do that was so bad? We'll never know the whole truth, but what we do know is that he was a primary author and promoter of the New World Order set forth in the new United Nations Charter, modeled after the Soviet Constitution, not the American Constitution. Think about that for a moment ... a lying Soviet communist spy in the Roosevelt administration set up the framework for the post war United Nations! No wonder it's such a mess today, mostly anti-American, anti-Israel—just like the communists planned it to be.

That was before and during the Great Depression. "They shared a belief that Marxist ideologies were the correct way to approach the problems of the ongoing Great Depression." In hindsight they were wrong, dead wrong for at least 100 million people, but at the time they couldn't know that.

The latter nineteenth century and early twentieth century were miserable times for many Americans, punctuated by the Great War (World War I) 1917, followed by the Spanish Flu pandemic 1918 where more U.S. soldiers died from the flu than were killed in battle during the war. Troops moving around the world in crowded ships and trains helped to spread the killer virus. Although the death toll attributed to the Spanish flu is often estimated at 20 million to 50 million victims worldwide, other estimates run as high as 100 million victims—around 3 percent of the world's population. This was followed by Prohibition (1920–1933), ten years later by the Great Depression (1929–1942), then widespread multi-year droughts and the Dust Bowl, followed closely by World War II. The Dust Bowl, also known as "the Dirty Thirties," **started in 1930 and lasted for about a decade,** but its long-term economic impacts on the region lingered much longer. The first half of the twentieth century was a time of the most severe weather events in modern America, with no help from industrial age CO2!

Chambers and many others thought their country had failed and now God, if there was one, had abandoned them too. These were all smart irreligious young people who hoped to make a difference, and were looking for something to believe in, something they'd be willing to die for. Communism seemed to be the answer for many of them since the religious old people, and their God, seemed to have let the country, and them personally, down. God didn't seem to care so they rejected God and turned to perfecting man and his institutions themselves. Communism has a formula for that. Same story when two young men named Karl Marx and Friedrich Engels wrote their *Communist Manifesto* in 1848 during equally trying times in Europe. History does tend to repeat itself, if we don't learn the lessons from it.

Lenin's Bolshevik Revolution (1917) had dethroned a totalitarian dictatorship and established a new system of social and economic justice for workers that had great appeal to American liberal elites and urban proletariats who viewed themselves as fellow sophisticates whose duty it was to save the little man from himself and his oppressors. The truth about the inevitable outcomes of socialism and communism were not yet evident, except inside Russia, the first country to put Marx's ideas into practice on a large scale.

With no internet, no satellite communications, no freedom of the press, propaganda churning out 24/7, purges of enemies, and no international air service, the West was unable to see the true nature and consequences of this new system until well after World War II. "Uncle Joe" Stalin was our ally but was working on his plan for world domination all the time.

Lenin referred to those card-carriers and sympathizers in America who dabbled fashionably with communism as "useful idiots," and only those willing to commit to going underground to spy for Moscow would be afforded the honor of being true revolutionary communists. Chambers, Ware, and Hiss were three of their best. Their MO was to serve in such a way as not to draw attention to themselves, blend in, go with the flow, infiltrate, influence, mold opinion, be helpful, pass documents to the party but discretely, no protests, marches, riots for these spies, leave that to the useful idiots. Keep a low profile, be inactive, if necessary, for years awaiting an opportunity to be of service to the cause of communism and worldwide peace and tranquility. Yes, some were in sleeper cells, just like in the movies ... *Manchurian Candidate, Deep State, Shadow Government* anyone? Saul Alinsky adopted this same strategy in his book *Rules for Radicals* which would become the playbook for new-left radicals in the 70s and beyond, including young Barack Obama and Hillary Clinton.

Roosevelt's New Deal, while I don't believe it was a socialist scheme to undermine America, nevertheless provided the ideal vehicle for these young intellectual communists to ply their trade, and not only did they flock to it, they were invited. The New Deal had all the elements of socialism. Liberals and communists have the same aims, that's why the forty-five goals discussed earlier sound like a liberal agenda but were produced by Soviet communists, pre-1958. It's also why liberals came to the defense of Alger Hiss. If he was exposed as having nefarious motives, they would be exposed because their beliefs and aims were the same. It would not matter that they did not share membership in the same political party. Liberals were democrats, Hiss was a communist. Same is true today, not all democrats are liberals/communists, some are simply "useful idiots," but all liberals/socialists/communists are democrats!

Felix Frankfurter who served on the Supreme Court from 1939 to 1962, personally encouraged Hiss to leave his law practice in New York and move to Washington DC to join the New Deal. Frankfurter also had gotten the young Harvard graduate, Hiss, a job law clerking for the famous Oliver Wendell Holmes. Hiss traveled in high circles, and yes, he was a Soviet communist spy!

In short, the Roosevelt administration and the following Truman administration, as well as Hollywood, News Media, academia, universities, unions, lawyers, business, and government were shot through with communist spies, not just useful idiots ... real spies!

Well that's interesting history but what does that have to do with me and my life and our country today? The Soviet Union is dissolved, America is the most powerful nation on earth, by a lot, so why worry?

The young intellectuals described above can perhaps be forgiven for falling for the siren calls of communism because they could not possibly know the outcome. BUT the intellectuals and students of today have no excuse for falling for the same, unless they are also useful idiots or true communists. I no longer buy Reagan's bone he threw to liberals in his time, that "it's not that our liberal friends are ignorant, it's that they know so much that isn't so." With the internet, Google, Amazon, and smart phones, there is no excuse for "knowing so much that isn't so," especially if you have read this book. Any person who can read this book and then vote for any democrat in 2020 might not only be ignorant, they might be a communist! Well, there is one other possibility … stupid, defined as willful ignorance.

Whittaker Chambers found God, recognized the evil that was communism, withdrew from the party and the underground and became an informer to the FBI and Congress as to what the communists of his day were up to.

The HUAC and the FBI ferreted out many communists in government, Hollywood, academia, business, and unions with help from Chambers, and others who saw the farce and failure of the CP in America and the Soviet Union. Senator Joe McCarthy came along later, after the Hiss–Chambers hearings. His obnoxious behavior and aggressive tactics brought disgrace to the true anti-communists of the day and Chambers wanted nothing to do with him. He was right about the communist infiltration of Hollywood and the U.S. government, but the smoke McCarthy generated eclipsed the factual and sincere witness Chambers proclaimed, much to the delight of liberals and communists of that day. Every liberal knows who Joe McCarthy is, few today know who Whittaker Chambers is. *The Witness and the President: Whittaker Chambers, Ronald Reagan*, K. Alan Snyder, PhD, Professor of History at Southeastern University, Lakeland, FL, 2015

The following are excerpts and my commentary from a book by one of the leading experts on Whittaker Chambers, Dr. Alan Snyder. I heard a presentation by Dr. Snyder on this subject at a civic club meeting about four years ago. At that time, I had never heard of Whittaker Chambers, but like most I sure had heard of Joe McCarthy and, of course, Ronald Reagan. I've always admired Reagan's speeches, a combination of humor, profound insights, and steadfast anti-communist fervor. The humor was all Reagan, the insights and anti-communist fervor came from his experiences in Hollywood combined with the testimony of Cleon Skousen, *The Naked Communist*, 1958, and the witness of Whittaker Chambers, *Witness*, 1952—both best sellers in their day.

I read *The Naked Communist* in 1975 and it changed my thinking about politics forever. Don't know how I missed it, but I'd never heard of *Witness* or Whittaker Chambers until I heard Professor Snyder speak. I bought the book that day and knew I'd use it someday.

> "#1 *New York Times* **best seller for thirteen consecutive weeks**, it was first published in 1952. *Witness* is the true story of Soviet spies in America and the trial that captivated a nation. Part literary effort, part philosophical treatise, this intriguing autobiography recounts the famous Alger Hiss case and reveals much more. Chambers' worldview and his belief that "man without mysticism is a monster" went on to help make political conservatism a national force."—Amazon

Following are reviews by a few credible sources most readers will recognize and respect:

> *"As long as humanity speaks of virtue and dreams of freedom, the life and writings of Whittaker Chambers will ennoble and inspire."* —PRESIDENT RONALD REAGAN

> *"One of the dozen or so indispensable books of the century..."* —GEORGE F. WILL

"*Witness changed my worldview, my philosophical perceptions, and, without exaggeration, my life.*" —ROBERT D. NOVAK,

from his Foreword:

"*Chambers has written one of the really significant American autobiographies. When some future Plutarch writes his American Life, he will find in Chambers penetrating and terrible insights into America in the early twentieth century.*" —ARTHUR SCHLESINGER

Why is this historic information so important for us to understand today?

A major theme of this book, *Repeal and Replace America*, is that the Democratic Party, spawn of Roosevelt Liberals, was hijacked by the ideology of Marxist communism in the early twentieth century and is now openly pursuing socialism, and socialism is distinctly Marxist. These are outrageous, offensive, and insulting claims … if not true! But they are true.

So what if these guys from the Depression age in the 30s and 40s were communist spies? That Soviet communists sought to infiltrate and spy on America for nefarious purposes is indisputable. What connects Marxist ideology with American liberalism is their remarkable similarity. Most democrats would say they are liberal not communist. Labels aside, it doesn't matter, if your aims and goals are the same. The forty-five goals, those not specifically relating to the Soviet Union, are all liberal positions, aims, and aspirations, not conservative values and certainly not traditionally American values.

SUMMARY AND CONCLUSION:
CLOSING ARGUMENT FOR THE CASE AGAINST THE LEFT FOR THEIR CLANDESTINE STRATEGY TO FUNDAMENTALLY TRANSFORM AMERICA INTO A SOCIALIST PARTOCRACY

The progressive left, represented at the ballot box in 2020 by the Democratic Socialist Party led by Barak Obama, Hillary Clinton, Nancy Pelosi, Chuck Schumer, Joe Biden, Bernie Sanders, AOC, and Omar, has a rich heritage of ideological evolution and revolution stretching all the way back to their patriarchs Karl Marx, Friedrich Engels, Nikolai Lenin, and Leon Trotsky. In the nineteenth century, democrats were the party of slavery; in the twentieth century they became the party of socialism. No economic systems in history have failed in every way like slavery and socialism. Socialism is the new Slavery! Yet in the twenty-first century, post-Kennedy democrats are openly declaring themselves to be democratic socialists and running on "the most progressive platform in American history," so says Barack Obama in his Biden endorsement video.

Attempting to "fundamentally transform America" into what they believe it should be by unconstitutional, unethical, illegal, and clandestine means, while pursing goals set down by our arch enemy, Soviet/Russian communism is a crime against America, and the forty-five goals is the smoking gun!

Following the goals created by Soviet communists and American Liberals for the destruction of America from the inside the left has, over the last sixty years, infiltrated the government, press, entertainment, academia, schools, courts, churches, unions, and big business, with devastating effects. That the goals and aims of the liberal progressive left, all democrats, came down from America's arch enemy, Soviet/Russian communism indicts the Democratic Party as being Un-American and unworthy to hold office or serve in government. The courts, many dominated by leftist infiltrators, will not render a just verdict, but hopefully the American patriots who vote in November will.

The conservative right, represented at the ballot box in 2020 by the Republican Party led by Donald J. Trump also has a rich heritage of ideological evolution and revolution stretching all the way back to its patriarchs George Washington, Thomas Jefferson, John Adams, and Alexander Hamilton. Trump has exposed the liberal press as "fake news," reduced taxes and regulations, built up the military, facilitated millions of new jobs, confounded liberal politicians, and unleashed the American entrepreneurial spirit to create the best economy and highest employment in our history. He is now leading a group of leading experts in government and the private sector to deal with the coronavirus pandemic, while the democrats carp and delay … hoping to use the situation against Trump even if it means economic depression and painful death of innocent Americans.

Do you really believe what you say? I believe there is no crime they are not willing to commit or at least condone, and no lie so big they are not willing to tell in order to get their way. Recent events have proven that to be true. So, yes, I absolutely believe that. Their attempted illegal and treasonous coup against our president is proof enough of their evil intent, and it was virtually unanimous!

Sometimes progress requires revolution, like in 1917 in Russia, or like in 2017 in America. From 1917 to 2017, a vast left-wing conspiracy of elites, ideologs, and activists who set out to change the world from what it was to what they believe it should be have come and gone across the political landscape of the world. The bloody consequences of all leftist/socialist revolutions across that hundred-year span, no matter what part of the globe, have consistently produced mutually shared poverty, tyranny, death, and destruction. The bloodless American revolution of 2017 has produced more prosperity, opportunity, freedom, safety, security, and confidence than at any time in American history.

It's time to stand up and be counted, which side are you on? Do your peers, co-workers, friends, and family know you are a pro-life, patriotic, Christian, conservative Trump supporter ... or what? Do you have the moral courage to defend your position in public? This book will give the reader ammunition to do so. At the very least be committed to quietly defeating this scourge of socialism at the ballot box and encouraging every conservative you know to do the same... VOTE REPUBLICAN, ANY REPUBLICAN, ALL REPUBLICAN!!!

The material presented and positions taken in this book will likely be controversial, insulting, and even offensive to partisan people suffering from Trump Derangement Syndrome (TDS) who are either committed leftists or useful idiots of the left, i.e., democrats ... so be it!

Everyone is entitled to their own opinion, but they are not entitled to their own facts. And the truth is totally independent of what a person believes about it. When a person or organization publicly pushes a position of consequence that is based on falsehoods and untruthful testimony, they deserve to be called out for it. And if they continue to push it, they deserve to be shamed and prosecuted for it. These people are all democrats, fake-news, liberal academia, etc.

As a scientist and pragmatist, I am a seeker of facts and truth, and when someone takes a public position which is counter to either, I feel like it is my obligation and duty to expose them, not because they disagree with me, but because they disagree with the facts and the truth, i.e., because they are wrong!

Facts are stubborn things, and the truth always comes out in the end. That is what we see happening now, but short being put in prison, it won't stop the left because to them lying and subterfuge is a skill of their trade, not a sin. Think Barack Obama, "you can keep your doctor", or Hillary Clinton, "Benghazi was a result of a video", or Adam Schiff, "evidence of Trump's collusion with Russia is in plain sight." These people can lie with such conviction it's almost believable

The liars, leakers, partisan hacks, and bleeding-heart liberals on the looney left, including some people the reader may know, well-meaning but misguided liberals, democrats in Congress, and organizations like the lamestream media and Hollywood, are being totally discredited as the truth and the facts come out. But they won't give up or admit it because their hypocrisy knows no bounds … they are shameless. The voters can shame them in November 2020 by reelecting Donald Trump and rubbing their noses in it!

SOME FINAL THOUGHTS FROM THE AUTHOR

I've devoted a lot of time and energy in this book explaining what I'm against and why. So, let me conclude with explaining what I'm for and why. If you are of like mind or even have an open mind, these points will bring clarity to the political choices we face in 2020.

Putting aside Trump's sometimes offensive personality and tweets and Biden's sometimes embarrassing dementia and gaffs, what kind of country do we want for ourselves and our posterity ... and is there a clear choice in 2020 that fits our vision for America?

What I want is a new contract with America, i.e., candidates for office in 2020 to tell us where they stand and what they will promise to address regarding the following priorities:

TAXES—reduced, revised tax code—everybody pays something, simplify filing

REGULATIONS—eliminated, job-killing regulations a top priority

ECONOMY—booming, especially blue collar

MILITARY—strengthened,   peace   through strength policy

CONGRESS reformed—term limits, no play/no pay, 401k, no pension, social security, market health care, work at least forty hours/week at Capital

DOJ/FBI/CIA/NSA DEEP STATE—offenders prosecuted and reputation restored

GOVERNMENT—shrunk; 401k replaces pensions, attrition, government unions banned

WELFARE STATE—replaced with OPPORTUNITY STATE with jobs/jobs/jobs

K-12 EDUCATION—returned to states, school choice, vouchers for parents

STUDENT LOAN PROGRAM—reformed, grants for qualified degree graduates, universities guarantee half the loan, no loans for useless degrees

BORDERS—secured, illegal invaders kept out, illegal criminals deported

SANCTUARY CITIES/STATES—prosecuted for aiding and abetting criminal aliens

REFUGEE RESETTLEMENT—restricted, no mandatory settlements in states

IMMIGRATION—laws enforced aggressively, lottery eliminated, merit-based visas only

BUSINESS—pro-business policies advanced, especially for small business

TRADE—deals revised, i.e., China, USMCA, U.K., E.U., South Korea, Japan, India

AMERICA FIRST—putting our country and our citizens first, but not isolationists

HEALTH CARE—enhanced, promote competition and innovation across state lines, allow co-ops, preexisting conditions universally covered, repeal ObamacarWe

RELIGION—respected and restored to public places, schools, government

ABORTION—Roe v. Wade overturned, let states decide otherwise

MARRIAGE—respected, traditional, one man + one woman

GENDER—acknowledged as biological, not political or social

ENVIRONMENT—stewarded; practice responsibility not radicalism

CLIMATE CHANGE ALARMISM—denied; adapt to natural change, not overreact

FIRST AMENDMENT—enforced; speech, religion, assembly, fake news exposed

SECOND AMENDMENT—defended and upheld, violent gun crimes prosecuted

HISTORY—preserved, stop statue removals, American history taught

JUDICIARY—packed with pro-life conservative, constitutional judges

LAW ENFORCEMENT—respected and supported, local, state, federal

CRIMINALS—incarcerated, differentiate violent and nonviolent offenders

CHINA—contained; stymy their progress militarily and economically

RUSSIA—restrained; sanctions strengthened

NORTH KOREA—contained, denuclearization, stop testing nukes and missiles

IRAN—bankrupted or destroyed

SPACE—explored and militarized; Space Force for military defense

EXECUTIVE BRANCH—purged of all Obama appointees and sympathizers

PENTAGON—purged of anti-Trumpers, Obama supporters

CIVIL RIGHTS—for conservatives enforced, violations prosecuted, civilly and criminally.

ANTI-AMERICAN ACTIVITIES—exposed; inside and outside government, UN challenged

Don't be fooled by another leftist scheme of the democrats, Soros, and their ilk. Vote Republican, any Republican in 2020.

Following is a chart I developed comparing conservative positions with liberal positions on the above topics. Where relevant I connected the specific communist goals for the destruction of America, previously discussed, with the appropriate liberal position, hand in glove!

Conservative Capitalist America	Liberal Socialist Amerika
LOWER TAXES—everyone pays something	HIGHER TAXES—Soak the "rich"
FEWER REGULATIONS—aggressive reduction in all areas of life and government	MORE REGULATIONS—aggressive increase in all areas of life and government
ECONOMY UNLEASHED—citizens in charge of progress, business unchained	ECONOMY CONTROLLED—government in charge of progressivism, businesses shackled
MILITARY STRENGTHENED	MILITARY WEAKENED AND DEPLETED
CONGRESS REFORMED—term limits	CONGRESS PROTECTED—cronyism
DOJ/FBI/CIA/NSA/FISA DEEP STATE—offenders prosecuted; reputation restored	DEEP STATE PROTECTED— to serve and secure the regime and its comrades; frame and prosecute its enemies, like Obama did!
FED GOVERNMENT—Shrunk; 401k replaces pensions, attrition 5%/year, government unions banned	FED GOVERNMENT—Expanded, new hiring, new bureaucracies, more rules and regulations.

WELFARE STATE CONTRACTED—Replaced with OPPORTUNITY STATE with jobs/jobs/jobs, work requirements, no aid to illegals.	WELFARE STATE EXPANDED— More food stamps, free stuff and subsidies to dependent democrat voting constituents, illegals included. No work requirements.
K-12 EDUCATION DE-FEDERALIZED—Returned to states, school choice, vouchers for parents, charter, faith-based, home schools supported, textbooks/curriculum are a local choice. Right-to-work rules for teachers who don't want to join a union.	K-12 EDUCATION FEDERALIZED—Run by Department of Education and NEA unions, textbooks and curriculum approved by Washington to reflect party doctrines. *Goal #17. Get control of the schools. Use them as transmission belts for socialism and current Communist propaganda. Soften the curriculum. Get control of teachers' associations. Put the party line in textbooks.* *Goal #18. Gain control of all student newspapers.*
STUDENT LOAN PROGRAM— Reformed, for tuition and books only; converted to grants for graduates in fields of demand, e.g., STEM. Colleges must insure half the loan. Tuitions at schools taking grant and loan money reduced by 20%.	FREE TUITION – For all, including illegals. All existing student loans forgiven, paid by taxpayers, printed money/ debt.

BORDERS— Secured, walls completed, illegal invaders kept out, illegal criminals deported. Coming to America is a privilege, not a right.	OPEN BORDERS— The U.S. is a sanctuary for all humanity … give us your tired, your poor, you down-trodden …and we will make loyal democrats out of them all. Ban border obstacles as voter suppression.
SANCTUARY CITIES/STATES— Prosecuted for aiding and abetting criminal aliens, failing to comply with federal law.	SANCTUARYS ENCOURAGED— ICE eliminated, Border Patrol kept at border, illegals get welfare and protection. Deportations ended, deportees returned, reunited with their families in the U.S., legal or illegal.
REFUGEE RESETTLEMENT PROGRAM—Reformed, limited, states and communities may opt out.	REFUGEE RESETTLEMENT PROGRAM—expanded, preference given to non-whites, Muslims, blacks. Feds and UN decide, states and communities have no say … as it is now!
IMMIGRATION—Laws enforced aggressively, merit-based visas only, illegal invaders returned immediately, banned permanently.	IMMIGRATION— Expanded, visas to favor likely dependent democrat voters, not independent educated professionals.

BUSINESS— Probusiness policies advanced, especially small business, regulations reduced, taxes cut, hands off approach, right-to-work	BUSINESS— Highly regulated, heavily taxed, force BOD makeup, unions protected, profits limited, salary structure controlled by Feds.
TRADE— Deals revised, reciprocal, fair, IP protected, i.e., China, USMCA, UK, EU, South Korea, Japan, India. America First	TRADE— Back room deals made which benefit the party, friends, and family of the President, quid pro Joe Biden. Globalism First
AMERICA FIRST— Putting our country and our citizens first, not isolationist but First among Winners. Illegal aliens are not American citizens and will not be rewarded above citizens, in any way. American exceptionalism has made America Great and we don't apologize for it.	AMERICA LAST— The U.S. is no better than any other country, we apologize for our exceptional arrogance and for using more than our fair share of resources and energy. We deserve to be Last among Losers and as good socialists in training, we will try harder.
HEALTH CARE— Enhanced free market care, promote competition and innovation across state lines, co-ops like Medishare, group policies, preexisting conditions guaranteed coverage in all plans.	MEDICARE-FOR-ALL— Single payer, government run. Private and company paid insurance banned.

RELIGION— Respected and restored to public places, schools, government. Acknowledge that without "Our Creator," we have no unalienable rights. Return voluntary prayer and Bible study to schools and public gatherings, acknowledge Christmas as Jesus Christ's birthday celebration. Acknowledge that our founders were religious people, 98% Protestant, and our Constitution was only "written for a moral and religious people and is wholly inadequate for any other." — John Adams	SEPARATION OF CHURCH AND STATE—Strictly enforced, statues removed, engravings obliterated, "In God We Trust," and "One Nation Under God" eliminated from all government buildings, pledges, money, courts, etc. Military bibles confiscated; chaplains replaced with psychologists. *Goal #28. Eliminate prayer or any phase of religious expression in the schools and the government on the grounds that it violates the principle of "separation of church and state."*
PRO-LIFE— Roe v. Wade overturned by Supreme Court, let states decide otherwise. Human life begins at conception, a biological fact. Abortion is taking human life, at any stage … but particularly egregious after the fetus is formed and able to feel pain. You make your choice when you decide to drop your drawers, everything after that is consequences and responsibility, which must be accepted, not shirked by slaughtering an innocent, albeit inconvenient, unborn child. God said to Jeremiah, "I knew you while you were still in the womb."	PRO-ABORTION— Abortion on demand, at any stage, up to and including the point of birth, or even after a live birth if you live in the new Peoples Republic of Virginia! This is a necessary tool to encourage the widespread consequences of: *Goal #25. Breakdown cultural standard of morality by promoting pornography and obscenity in books, magazines, motion pictures, radio and TV.* *Goal #26. Present… degeneracy and promiscuity as "normal, natural, and healthy."*

MARRIAGE & FAMILY— Traditional, one man + one woman. Government policies should financially encourage marriage and two-parent families, not promote and reward promiscuity, single parent homes, and easy divorce … as is done now. Started with LBJs Great Society which has decimated the black family and culture.	MARRIAGE & FAMILY— Continue the breakdown of the American two-parent family to create the disfunction, disunity, and immorality needed to bring down existing institutions and prepare people for a Marxist utopia to follow. *Goals #40. Discredit the family as an institution. Encourage promiscuity and easy divorce.* *Goal #41. Emphasize the need to raise children away from the negative influence of parents Attribute prejudices, mental blocks and retarding of children to suppressive influence of parents.*
GENDER— Acknowledged as biological, not political or social. Athletic competition, military service, and other physically demanding activities based on biological gender, not gender preference. Separate showers and bathrooms for girls and boys. No taxpayer funded gender changes.	TRANS-GENDER— Recognized as normal, natural, healthy … a personal choice regardless of birth condition. Parents and schools forbidden from forcing gender identification on children. Made a protected class, like sexual orientation. Taxpayer, including single payer insurance funded gender changes on demand.

ENVIRONMENT STEWARDSHIP—Clean air, water, soil, and oceans a priority but balanced with cost/benefit considerations, including jobs and national security. CO2 declared by Supreme Court not to be a pollutant, but the life of plants, not to be regulated by EPA and the Clean Air Act. Hold a national trial on Climate Change Alarmism giving both sides equal time and resources to prepare.	ENVIRONMENTALISM — Environmental stewardship with a political agenda; radical environmentalism taxpayer funded, EPA expanded, given new powers to regulate every aspect of human life. Waters of the U.S. Rule, Clean Power Plan, others revived regardless of cost. Endangered species act expanded to allow Sierra Club, Greenpeace, others to shut down development.
CLIMATE CHANGE ALARMISM—Alarmism denied and exposed for the fraud and scam it is. Promote adaptation to real climate change, with real science, by real experts, not bureaucrats and profs on the dole. Cost/Benefit Analysis considered in any proposed actions.	CLIMATE CHANGE ALARMISM—Green New Deal passed, Paris Climate Accord reinstated, decarbonization of the planet a goal. Costs are no obstacle; we must act to save the world even if it means economic suicide for America. Supported by Biden, Al Gore, and Bill Gates, so it must be a good thing.

FIRST AMENDMENT FOR ALL — Freedom of speech, religion, assembly, petition assured for conservatives, Violators prosecuted as civil rights violations to fullest extent of the law. Lawsuits seeking monetary damages filed. Fed grants to institutions violating conservative's rights withdrawn.	FIRST AMENDMENT FOR LEFT ONLY—Liberals say and do whatever they please, especially to conservatives who don't deserve respect. Left never pays a price, never gets prosecuted, above the law. Conservative students bullied and force-fed liberalism by tenured professors.
SECOND AMENDMENT— Defended. Gun violence prosecuted aggressively. National concealed carry encourages citizens to defend themselves from criminals before the law arrives to investigate their murder. NRA, Gun Owners of America, gun manufacturers considered a national treasure and given due respect.	SECOND AMENDMENT— Repealed or neutered. Confuse the public by conflating gun safety with gun violence. Ban semi-auto weapons, tax ammunition out of existence, license all gun owners, then ultimately confiscate their guns, by force if necessary, like every socialist partocracy in history has done.

AMERICAN HISTORY— Preserved. Stop statue removals and historical revisionism, teach America history in all schools. Emphasize the foundational principles in the Declaration of Independence and the Constitution, and how the United States of America invented freedom not slavery, and has become the greatest nation the world has ever known through life, liberty, and the pursuit of happiness, and Ronald Reagan and Donald Trump are the two best presidents we've ever had, and Jimmy Carter and Barack Obama are tied for the worst ... LBJ a close third!	AMERICAN HISTORY— Reviled, revised, rejected *Goals #30. Discredit the American founding fathers. Present them as selfish aristocrats who had no concern for the "common man."* *Goal #31. Belittle all forms of American culture and discourage the teaching of American history on the ground that it was only a minor part of "the big picture."* Paint American history as racist, sexist, xenophobic, homophobic, hateful, irredeemable, deplorable— you know, Hillary's list.
FEDERAL JUDICIARY— Packed, with young conservative textualist and originalist constitutional scholars for life. Preference for Pro-lifers willing to reverse Roe v. Wade.	FEDERAL JUDICIARY— Packed with liberal, pro-abortion, anti-constitutional lawyers who will legislate liberal causes from the bench; and *Goal #29. Discredit the American Constitution by calling it inadequate, old-fashioned, out of step with modern needs, a hindrance to cooperation between nations on a world-wide basis.* *Goal #16. Use technical decisions of the courts to weaken basic American institutions by claiming their activities violate rights.*

LAW ENFORCEMENT— Supported, Respected, Admired	LAW ENFORCEMENT— Suspected, Resisted, Reviled
"Blue Lives Matter More Than Black Lies and Communist Spies."	"Pigs in a blanket, fry 'em like bacon" *Goal #42. Create the impression that violence and insurrection are legitimate aspects of the American tradition; that students and special-interest groups should rise up and use "united force" to solve economic, political or social problems.*
CRIMINALS—Incarcerated, differentiate between violent and non-violent offenders. Encourage adult citizens to carry a concealed weapon, get trained, and to take out (stop the attack of) violent offenders who threaten their, or others, lives, or are committing a forcible felony. Florida Statue Chapter 790 and 776 makes it legal. Polk County Sherriff Grady Judd's team of deputies teach Concealed Weapons Permit, Active Assailant Response, and Self-defense classes routinely and encourage citizens to learn to defend themselves because when seconds count, minutes don't matter. Don't be a victim!	CRIMINALS—Soft on criminals, hard on legal law-abiding gun owners. Criminals are just victims of the failure of American institutions and society in general to show compassion and treat them equally. Blacks and Hispanics are overly represented in the prison population proving the racist nature of the legal system.

CHINA, RUSSIA, NORTH KOREA— Stymie their progress by aggressive economic, diplomatic, and military means.	CHINA, RUSSIA, NORTH KOREA— Be nice, don't upset them, be careful, appease them so they may play nice. Cut deals that fill the pockets of our family and friends, like quid pro Joe did.
IRAN— Bankrupt them with sanctions, use military force if necessary, make them pay a heavy price for terrorism. Don't let them get a nuclear bomb.	IRAN— Return to nuclear deal Obama, Biden, and Kerry negotiated, remove sanctions, hope they don't get a nuclear bomb on our watch. Throw Israel under the bus.
SPACE— Reestablish the manned spaceflight program and a new military Space Force. Establish a Star Wars type Federation among NATO allies (excluding Turkey) to challenge the Evil Empire of Russia, China, Iran, North Korea.	SPACE— Return to Obama's NASA program, no manned flight, use money for liberal domestic priorities; make one of the new Administrator's priorities outreach to Muslims … like Obama did.
EXECUTIVE BRANCH— Purge all divisions of all Obama appointees and all identifiable anti-Trump republicans … including DOJ, FBI, CIA, NSA, DNI, DOD, DOE, EPA, IRS, Secret Service, Pentagon, Whitehouse staff.	EXECUTIVE BRANCH— Purge all divisions of all republican appointees and any identifiable pro-Trump democrats … including DOJ, FBI, CIA, NSA, DNI, DOD, DOE, EPA, IRS, Secret Service, Pentagon, Whitehouse staff…like Bill Clinton and Obama did when they took office. Clinton's AG Janet Reno fired 63 of 64 U.S. Attorneys on day 1.

ANTI-AMERICAN ACTIVITIES—Identify all anti-American activists, countries, agents, and organizations and make them change their ways or pay a steep price. Demand they pay their fair share and use American taxpayer's money responsibly and effectively. Including in the UN, WHO, World Bank, World Trade Organization, NATO.	ANTI-AMERICAN ACTIVIES— Identify all anti-American activists, countries, and actors and make them pay a steep price ... to me, quid pro Joe and my family and friends! *Goal #12. Resist any attempt to outlaw the Communist Party.* *Goal #13. Do away with all loyalty oaths.* *Goal #15. Capture one or both political parties in the United States.*
UNITED NATIONS— Identify all nations who vote against the U.S. and punish them, hold them accountable...like Nikki Haley said. Support Israel and counter Iran. Make other nations pay their fair share or withdraw our money proportionately.	UNITED NATIONS— Submit the U.S. to UN authority and support its charter, written by Soviet spy Alger Hiss, as superior to the U.S. Constitution. *Goal #11. Promote the U.N. as the only hope for mankind. If its charter is rewritten, demand that it is set up as one-world government with its own independent armed forces.*
THE MEDIA— Continue to call out and denigrate the hostile corrupt anti-American press as Fake News. Use Twitter, Fox, and OAN to get the truth out to the people.	THE MEDIA— Use the compliant media as a propaganda arm to push our liberal narrative on an unsuspecting public. *Goal #20. Infiltrate the press. Get control of book-review assignments, editorial writing, and policy-making positions.* *Goal #21. Gain control of key positions in radio, TV and pictures.*

ART and CULTURE— Let people who enjoy art and culture pay for it, e.g., Kennedy Center, not taxpayers. Preserve our national statues, art, cultural sites which have natural and traditional beauty and value.	ART and CULTURE— Use art, culture, and entertainment to divide citizens by class, remove historical statues as racist, promote vile grotesque images as "modern" art. *Goal #22. Continue discrediting American culture. An American Communist cell was told to "eliminate all good sculpture from parks and building, substitute shapeless, awkward and meaningless forms."* *Goal #23. Control art critics and directors of art museums. "Our plan it to promote ugliness, repulsive meaningless art."*
SOCIALISM— Rejected as incompatible with America's constitution and way of life in a free enterprise market-driven economy of maximum personal liberty.	SOCIALISM— Embraced as the only fair solution to the evils of capitalism and Americanism *Goal #32. Support any socialist movement to give centralized control over any part of the culture – education, social agencies, welfare programs, mental health clinics, etc.* *Goal #33. Eliminate all laws or procedures which interfere with the operation of the Communist apparatus.*

And with that I'll close this 2020 edition with a Jeff Foxworthyism..

"If you can read this book with an open mind and still vote for a democrat in 2020, you just might be a communist!"… or at least a useful idiot!

If Trump is reelected, I plan to publish a second edition as an update in the spring of 2022 before the midterm elections, during President Trump's second term. This edition will provide an update on the ongoing investigations and prosecutions of the Obama conspirators, outcome of the coronavirus pandemic (a health crisis), and the coronavirus plandemic (a China/democrat political scheme to take down the president and America), the June anarchy and riots and following occupy movements, and dredging the swamp which will start the day after the election in November.

Following is a bonus read ... a Facebook post/essay written by me in 2019 before the pandemic. Having made a strong case against the democrats, it is appropriate to express why I support the current alternative.

MY CASE FOR TRUMP

"My purpose in writing this essay is to question how so many otherwise intelligent normal people can feel so viscerally negative about a man who has done so much to enable us, through our own initiatives, not government bailouts or subsidies, to reclaim America from the past sixteen years of Bush's and Obama's bad judgement and destructive policies, foreign and domestic. The alternative, crooked Hillary Clinton, was to me unthinkably disastrous and more of the same, except I believe she would have consolidated the deep state assets in the FBI, CIA, Pentagon, NSA, etc. around her personally, and the country would be ruled by her for a generation. I think it would have been the end of our constitutional republic as we've known it ... or the beginning of a new civil war.

So, with the economy booming due to Trump-led tax cuts and regulation reductions, with lowest unemployment and highest GDP growth in decades, the EPA being reigned in from decades of bureaucratic overreach, the depleted military being massively rebuilt and destroying the ISIS caliphate due to Trump's leadership, North Korea's nuclear ambitions curtailed, China being challenged for decades of egregious unfair trade behavior, Russia being sanctioned and it's enemies armed with lethal weapons, withdrawal from the disastrous and one-sided Iran Nuclear Deal followed by crippling sanctions and military threats to Iran which will ultimately bankrupt the evil Islamic regime, withdrawal from the costly and feckless

Paris Climate Accord which would have crippled our economy and sent trillions of taxpayer dollars overseas to countries like India and China with little to no impact on the climate, doing everything possible, with no help from democrats in Congress, to stop illegal immigration and its associated costs to our society, proposing a rational merit-based immigration system, eliminating the Obamacare mandate and except for John McCain, would have repealed and replaced it entirely, and much much more, all in two-and-a-half years while under siege by Obama's shadow government, spies, and covert operatives, but after 30 million dollars of investigation ... NO COLLUSION, NO OBSTRUCTION ... and drawing no salary in the process!!!!

If you only watch the mainstream media and listen to National Public Radio (NPR), with 92 percent negative coverage 24/7 of all things Trump, and you don't do your own research, you would naturally see Trump as the anti-Christ, as they do. If you want to know the real Donald J. Trump, read "Trump Revealed" 2016, commissioned by Jeff Bezos, Amazon CEO and owner of *the Washington Post*, no fans of Trump. Bob Woodward announced on MSNBC's Morning Joe in the spring of 2016 that there would be two books commissioned, spare no expenses ... one on Trump, one on Clinton. The Clinton book never came out. When the Trump book was reviewed on Morning Joe months later by the two main authors, Mika and Joe were so disappointed, it has never been mentioned again ... NO Collusion, NO Obstruction, NO Corruption ... just a hard-driving blue-collar billionaire who never gives up, never gives in, never quits ... insists on winning, winning, winning!!!

Renowned historian and author Victor Davis Hansen of Stanford wrote his own version, *The Case for Trump*, which inspired this essay

The next book and sequel should be named *Trump Unleashed* as he breaks the bonds of all these stupid investigations, gets the wind behind his back, and starts seriously dredging, not just draining, the swamp.

Having watched Trump in office now for two-and-a-half years, I'll acknowledge that Trump can be arrogant, egotistical, vain, abrasive, abusive, vulgar, vindictive, and every other nasty quality you don't want you children to adopt. He's no Ronald Reagan that's for sure, but I believe he has a good heart and loves America, and most importantly highly effective! And he's not the type of man we could take a series of in the White House, but he's who we need at this point in time. Lincoln was advised not to hire U.S. Grant because he was a drunk and a womanizer. Lincoln said, "I know that, but can he fight? Lincoln needed Grant to win the war against slavery and we need Trump to win the war against socialism.

Will you let your disdain for some of Trump's behaviors and mannerisms overshadow all he's done for us, and what he saved us from? In my view that would be pretty shallow. Think of it this way … a normal, nice, congenial politician, like Mike Pence or Mitt Romney, could not have beaten crooked Hillary Clinton and the democrats' dirty tricks machine. Even feisty war hero John McCain was trounced … we tried that twice before remember!

We need four more years of this brilliant patriotic New York street fighter named Trump to stabilize our economy, our military, our government …our republic!

As Bill Bennet recently said, "Sometimes you need a Mother Teresa and other times you need Dirty Harry. Trump just said that if we are attacked, it would mean the 'official end of Iran' … make my day punk! Same goes for Little Rocket Man! They believe he means it, so do I." —Facebook Post by the Author in May 2019

More on MY CASE FOR TRUMP:

Below are some of President Trumps actions and accomplishments. Consider these when you vote in November:

- Trump recently signed 3 bills to benefit Native people. One gives compensation to the Spokane tribe for loss of their lands in the mid-1900s, one funds Native language programs, and the third gives federal recognition to the Little Shell Tribe of Chippewa Indians in Montana.

- Trump finalized the creation of Space Force as our 6th Military branch.

- Trump signed a law to make cruelty to animals a federal felony so that animal abusers face tougher consequences.

- Violent crime has fallen every year he's been in office after rising during the 2 years before he was elected.

- Trump signed a bill making CBD and Hemp legal.

- Trump's EPA gave $100 million to fix the water infrastructure problem in Flint, Michigan.

- Under Trump's leadership, in 2018 the U.S. surpassed Russia and Saudi Arabia to become the world's largest producer of crude oil.

- Trump signed a law ending the gag orders on Pharmacists that prevented them from sharing money-saving information.

- Trump signed the "Allow States and Victims to Fight Online Sex Trafficking Act" (FOSTA), which includes the "Stop Enabling Sex Traffickers Act" (SESTA) which both give law enforcement and victims new tools to fight sex trafficking.

- Trump signed a bill to require airports to provide spaces for breastfeeding Moms.

- The 25% lowest-paid Americans enjoyed a 4.5% income boost in November 2019, which outpaces a 2.9% gain in earnings for the country's highest-paid workers.

- Low-wage workers are benefiting from higher minimum wages and from corporations that are increasing entry-level pay.

- Trump signed the biggest wilderness protection & conservation bill in a decade and designated 375,000 acres as protected land.

- Trump signed the Save our Seas Act which funds $10 million per year to clean tons of plastic & garbage from the ocean.

- He signed a bill this year allowing some drug imports from Canada so that prescription prices would go down.

- Trump signed an executive order this year that forces all healthcare providers to disclose the cost of their services so that Americans can comparison shop and know how much less providers charge insurance companies.

- When signing that bill, he said no American should be blindsided by bills for medical services they never agreed to in advance.

- Hospitals will now be required to post their standard charges for services, which include the discounted price a hospital is willing to accept.

- In the eight years prior to President Trump's inauguration, prescription drug prices increased by an average of 3.6% per year. Under Trump, drug prices have seen year-over-year declines in nine of the last ten months, with a 1.1% drop as of the most recent month.

- He created a White House VA Hotline to help veterans and principally staffed it with veterans and direct family members of veterans.

- VA employees are being held accountable for poor performance, with more than 4,000 VA employees removed, demoted, and suspended so far.

- Issued an executive order requiring the Secretaries of Defense, Homeland Security, and Veterans Affairs to submit a joint plan to provide veterans access to access to mental health treatment as they transition to civilian life.

- Because of a bill signed and championed by Trump, In 2020, most federal employees will see their pay increase by an average of 3.1% — the largest raise in more than 10 years.

- Trump signed into a law up to 12 weeks of paid parental leave for millions of federal workers.

- Trump administration will provide HIV prevention drugs for free to 200,000 uninsured patients per year for 11 years.

- Record sales during the 2019 holidays.

- Trump signed an order allowing small businesses to group together when buying insurance to get a better price

- President Trump signed the Preventing Maternal Deaths Act that provides funding for states to develop maternal mortality reviews to better understand maternal complications and identify solutions & largely focuses on reducing the higher mortality rates for Black Americans.

- In 2018, President Trump signed the groundbreaking First Step Act, a criminal justice bill which enacted reforms that make our justice system fairer and help former inmates successfully return to society.

- The First Step Act's reforms addressed inequities in sentencing laws that disproportionately harmed Black Americans and reformed mandatory minimums that created unfair outcomes.

- The First Step Act expanded judicial discretion in sentencing of non-violent crimes.

- Over 90% of those benefitting from the retroactive sentencing reductions in the First Step Act are Black Americans.

- The First Step Act provides rehabilitative programs to inmates, helping them successfully rejoin society and not return to crime.

- Trump increased funding for Historically Black Colleges and Universities (HBCUs) by more than 14%.

- Trump signed legislation forgiving Hurricane Katrina debt that threatened HBCUs.

- New single-family home sales are up 31.6% in October 2019 compared to just one year ago.

- Made HBCUs a priority by creating the position of executive director of the White House Initiative on HBCUs.

- Trump received the Bipartisan Justice Award at a historically black college for his criminal justice reform accomplishments.

- The poverty rate fell to a 17-year low of 11.8% under the Trump administration as a result of a jobs-rich environment.

- Poverty rates for African Americans and Hispanic-Americans have reached their lowest levels since the U.S. began collecting such data.

- President Trump signed a bill that creates five national monuments, expands several national parks, adds 1.3 million acres of wilderness, and permanently reauthorizes the Land and Water Conservation Fund.

- Trump's USDA committed $124 Million to rebuild rural water infrastructure.

- Consumer confidence & small business confidence is at an all-time high.

- More than 7 million jobs created since election.

- More Americans are now employed than ever recorded before in our history.

- More than 400,000 manufacturing jobs created since his election.

- Trump appointed 5 openly gay ambassadors.

- Trump ordered Ric Grinnell, his openly gay ambassador to Germany, to lead a global initiative to decriminalize homosexuality across the globe.

- Through Trump's Anti-Trafficking Coordination Team (ACTeam) initiative, Federal law enforcement more than doubled convictions of human traffickers and increased the number of defendants charged by 75% in ACTeam districts.

- In 2018, the Department of Justice (DOJ) dismantled an organization that was the internet's leading source of prostitution-related advertisements resulting in sex trafficking.

- Trump's OMB published new anti-trafficking guidance for government procurement officials to more effectively combat human trafficking.

- Trump's Immigration and Customs Enforcement's Homeland Security Investigations arrested 1,588 criminals associated with Human Trafficking.

- Trump's Department of Health and Human Services provided funding to support the National Human Trafficking Hotline to identify perpetrators and give victims the help they need.

- The hotline identified 16,862 potential human trafficking cases.

- Trump's DOJ provided grants to organizations that support human trafficking victims – serving nearly 9,000 cases from July 1, 2017, to June 30, 2018.

- The Department of Homeland Security has hired more victim assistance specialists, helping victims get resources and support.

- President Trump has called on Congress to pass school choice legislation so that no child is trapped in a failing school because of his or her zip code.

- The President signed funding legislation in September 2018 that increased funding for school choice by $42 million.

- The tax cuts signed into law by President Trump promote school choice by allowing families to use 529 college savings plans for elementary and secondary education.

- Under his leadership ISIS has lost most of their territory and been largely dismantled.

- ISIS leader Abu Bakr Al-Baghdadi was killed.

- Signed the first Perkins CTE reauthorization since 2006, authorizing more than $1 billion for states each year to fund vocational and career education programs.

- Executive order expanding apprenticeship opportunities for students and workers.

- Trump issued an Executive Order prohibiting the U.S. government from discriminating against Christians or punishing expressions of faith.

- Signed an executive order that allows the government to withhold money from college campuses deemed to be anti-Semitic and who fail to combat anti-Semitism.

- President Trump ordered a halt to U.S. tax money going to international organizations that fund or perform abortions.

- Trump imposed sanctions on the socialists in Venezuela who have killed their citizens.

- Finalized new trade agreement with South Korea.

- Made a deal with the European Union to increase U.S. energy exports to Europe.

- Withdrew the U.S. from the job killing TPP deal.

- Secured $250 billion in new trade and investment deals in China and $12 billion in Vietnam.

- Okayed up to $12 billion in aid for farmers affected by unfair trade retaliation.

- Has had over a dozen US hostages freed, including those Obama could not get freed.

- Trump signed the Music Modernization Act, the biggest change to copyright law in decades.

- Trump secured Billions that will fund the building of a wall at our southern border.

- The Trump Administration is promoting second chance hiring to give former inmates the opportunity to live crime-free lives and find meaningful employment.

- Trump's DOJ and the Board of Prisons launched a new "Ready to Work Initiative" to help connect employers directly with former prisoners.

- President Trump's historic tax cut legislation included new Opportunity Zone Incentives to promote investment in low-income communities across the country.

- 8,764 communities across the country have been designated as Opportunity Zones.

- Opportunity Zones are expected to spur $100 billion in long-term private capital investment in economically distressed communities across the country.

- Trump directed the Education Secretary to end Common Core.

- Trump signed the 9/11 Victims Compensation Fund into law.

- Trump signed measure funding prevention programs for Veteran suicide.

- Companies have brought back over a TRILLION dollars from overseas because of the TCJA bill that Trump signed.

- Manufacturing jobs are growing at the fastest rate in more than 30 years.

- Stock Market has reached record highs.

- Median household income has hit highest level ever recorded.

- African American unemployment is at an all-time low.

- Hispanic-American unemployment is at an all-time low.

- Asian-American unemployment is at an all-time low.

- Women's unemployment rate is at a 65-year low.

- Youth unemployment is at a 50-year low.

- We have the lowest unemployment rate ever recorded.

- The Pledge to America's Workers has resulted in employers committing to train more than 4 million Americans.

- 95 percent of U.S. manufacturers are optimistic about the future— the highest ever.

- As a result of the Republican tax bill, small businesses will have the lowest top marginal tax rate in more than 80 years.

- Record number of regulations eliminated that hurt small businesses.

- Signed welfare reform requiring able-bodied adults who don't have children to work or look for work if they're on welfare.

- Under Trump, the FDA approved more affordable generic drugs than ever before in history.

- Reformed Medicare program to stop hospitals from overcharging low-income seniors on their drugs—saving seniors 100's of millions of $$$ this year alone.

- Signed Right-To-Try legislation allowing terminally ill patients to try experimental treatment that wasn't allowed before.

- Secured $6 billion in new funding to fight the opioid epidemic.

- Signed VA Choice Act and VA Accountability Act, expanded VA telehealth services, walk-in-clinics, and same-day urgent primary and mental health care.

- U.S. oil production recently reached all-time high so we are less dependent on oil from the Middle East.

- The U.S. is a net natural gas exporter for the first time since 1957.

- NATO allies increased their defense spending because of his pressure campaign.

- Withdrew the United States from the job-killing Paris Climate Accord in 2017 and that same year the U.S. still led the world by having the largest reduction in Carbon emissions.

- Has his circuit court judge nominees being confirmed faster than any other new administration.

- Had his Supreme Court Justice's Neil Gorsuch and Brett Kavanaugh confirmed.

- Moved U.S. Embassy in Israel to Jerusalem.

- Agreed to a new trade deal with Mexico & Canada that will increase jobs here and $$$ coming in.

- Reached a breakthrough agreement with the E.U. to increase U.S. exports.

- Imposed tariffs on China in response to China's forced technology transfer, intellectual property theft, and their chronically abusive trade practices, has agreed to a Part One trade deal with China.

- Signed legislation to improve the National Suicide Hotline.

- Signed the most comprehensive childhood cancer legislation ever into law, which will advance childhood cancer research and improve treatments.

- The Tax Cuts and Jobs Act signed into law by Trump doubled the maximum amount of the child tax credit available to parents and lifted the income limits so more people could claim it.

- It also created a new tax credit for other dependents.

- In 2018, President Trump signed into law a $2.4 billion funding increase for the Child Care and Development Fund, providing a total of $8.1 billion to States to fund child care for low-income families.

- The Child and Dependent Care Tax Credit (CDCTC) signed into law by Trump provides a tax credit equal to 20-35% of child care expenses, $3,000 per child & $6,000 per family + Flexible Spending Accounts (FSAs) allow you to set aside up to $5,000 in pre-tax $ to use for child care.

- In 2019 President Donald Trump signed the Autism Collaboration, Accountability, Research, Education and Support Act (CARES) into law which allocates $1.8 billion in funding over the next five years to help people with autism spectrum disorder and to help their families.

- In 2019 President Trump signed into law two funding packages providing nearly $19 million in new funding for Lupus specific research and education programs, as well an additional $41.7 billion in funding for the National Institutes of Health (NIH), the most Lupus funding EVER.

- Another upcoming accomplishment to add: In the next week or two Trump will be signing the first major anti-robocall law in decades called the TRACED Act (Telephone Robocall Abuse Criminal Enforcement and Deterrence.) Once it is the law, the TRACED Act will extend the period of time the FCC has to catch & punish those who intentionally break telemarketing restrictions. The bill also requires voice service providers to develop a framework to verify calls are legitimate before they reach your phone.

- US stock market continually hits all-time record highs.

- Because so many people asked for a document with all of this listed in one place, here it is. No links provided to remove bias as Google search is easy. Print this out for family, friends, neighbors, etc. I encourage you to drop this list off to voters before the 2020 election too!

Trump did all of this while fighting flagrant abuse and impeachment charges.

Thank you for taking your time to read my book. If you think it would be a good read for friends and neighbors who may be on the fence, or need their convictions bolstered, please order multiple copies and pass them around.

Sincerely,

Jim Spurlock, MS Applied Physics, husband, father, grandfather, pro-life Christian conservative patriot who will vote to reelect the most effective president in modern times, Donald J. Trump!

Contact the author at Repeal.Replace.America@gmail.com Notice the dots between words.

APPENDIX

The following are some of the books that have influenced my worldview over the years and are incorporated and referenced in relevant part in this work. These books combined tell a story, a story of subterfuge, corruption, infiltration, spying, lying, leaking, loathing, and treason by the left to transform America from what it is, a religious capitalist republic, to what they believe it should be, an irreligious socialist partocracy run by them. This book, *Repeal and Replace America—The Left's Strategy to Fundamentally Transform America*, connects the dots across a century of activism, from 1917, Nicolai Lenin, the Bolshevik Revolution, through 2017, Donald Trump and the Deplorable Revolution.

The foundation of all leftist movements, including the new-left democrat party 1964–2020, now democratic socialists, is described in the first book below. The most thorough and profound exposure of the progressive left's motives and plans to transform America is in the second.

> *The Communist Manifesto: The Revolutionary Economic, Political, and Social Treatise That Has Transfigured the World*, Karl Marx and Friedrich Engels, 1848. This pamphlet, less than hundred pages, has had more influence on humankind that any book in history, except perhaps the Bible. But in Marx's case, all negative, since over 100 million people have been killed enforcing his theories

of economic socialism and social justice around the world. Marxism is a leftist ideology; not all democrats are Marxists, but all Marxists are democrats, or worse.

The Naked Communist: Exposing Communism and Restoring Freedom, by W. Cleon Skousen, 1958 and 1971 editions. Exposing the forty-five goals of Soviet communism for the destruction of America from within, Skousen's book became the textbook for the FBI and CIA in understanding the existential threat America faced. They are all not-so-coincidentally "liberal" ideas now adopted and blessed by the democrat party. Not all democrats are liberals, but all liberals are democrats, or worse.

Rules for Radicals: A Pragmatic Primer for Realistic Radicals, Saul D. Alinsky, 1971. Alinsky, a communist sympathizer in the 50s, developed the "community organizer" model used by Barack Obama and Hillary Clinton in their rise to power.

The Vast Left-Wing Conspiracy: The Untold Story of How Democratic Operatives, Eccentric Billionaires, Liberal Activists, and Assorted Celebrities Tried to Bring Down a President – and Why They'll Try Even Harder Next Time, by Byron York, National Review White House Correspondent, 2005.

The Shadow Party: How George Soros, Hillary Clinton, and Sixties Radicals Seized Control of the Democratic Party, by David Horowitz and Richard Poe, 2006. A *New York Times* Best Seller.

The Professors: The 101 Most Dangerous Academics in America, David Horowitz, 2006. Horowitz exposes the most Marxist professors in American universities and how they are influencing our young students, like those at Columbia did to Whittaker Chambers in the 20s and Barack Obama in the 80s.

Signature in the Cell: DNA and the Evidence for Intelligent Design, Stephen Meyer, 2009. This work is the first book to make a comprehensive case for Intelligent Design based upon DNA. Meyer investigates current evolutionary theories and the evidence that ultimately lead him to affirm Intelligent Design.

The Black Book of the American Left: The Collective Conservative Writings of David Horowitz, a Former Communist Radical, 2015

Big Agenda: President Trump's Plan to Save America, a *New York Times* Best Seller, David Horowitz, 2017

Secret Empires: How the America Political Class Hides Corruption and Enriches Family and Friends, Peter Schweizer, 2018. This book exposes how, because his father, VP Joe, was point man for Obama on Ukraine, Hunter Biden, and John Kerry's stepson obtained lucrative positions on the board of a Ukraine Oil and Gas company when they had no experience or skills, and then Joe Biden black mailed the Ukraine president to fire the prosecutor who was investigating the company his son worked for.

Dark Agenda: The War to Destroy Christian America, by David Horowitz, 2018. "Most Compelling Defense of Christianity" —Gov. Mike Huckabee

The Witness and the President: Whittaker Chambers, Ronald Reagan, & the Future of Freedom, K. Alan Snyder, 2015. The strange tale of Whittaker Chambers' conversion to communism, rejection of God, and back again. Also, of his testimony to the House Unamerican Activities Committee exposing Soviet spying withing the federal government, e.g., Alger Hiss and others. Ronald Regan was a huge fan and admirer of Chambers and many of his speeches contain the words of Chambers from his famous book, *Witness.* Chambers, perhaps more than any other person, inspired Reagan's war on communism from Hollywood to the Whitehouse, and is arguably can be indirectly credited with the fall of the Soviet Union shortly following Regan's second term as president.

Liberalism: How to Turn Good Men into Whiners, Weenies, and Wimps, Burgess Owens, 2016. Owens, former NFL starter, writes about the history of the cultural genocide perpetrated against black men and families by Lyndon Johnson's Great Society and democrats ever since to coopt their votes. He testified to Congress that it is democrats who owe reparations to the surviving black community today, for what they have done and not done.

If You Can Keep It: The Forgotten Promise of American Liberty, Eric Mataxis, a *New York Times* Best Seller, 2016. When Ben Franklin emerged from the Constitutional Convention a citizen asked him if we had a monarchy or a republic. Franklin replied, "A Republic, if you can keep it!"

Trump Revealed: An American Journey of Ambition, Ego, Money, and Power, Michael Kranish and Marc Fisher, Washington Post Journalists given a mission from Jeff Bezos, Amazon CEO and owner of the Post, to destroy Trump before the 2016 election. According to Bob Woodward on MSNBC Morning Joe, Bezos commissioned two books during the spring of 2016, one on Trump, one on Hillary. The one of Hillary never came out, the one on Trump was a flop and never mentioned again, but I read it!

Rediscovering Americanism:– And the Tyranny of Progressivism, Mark Levin, #1 *New York Times* Best Selling Author, 2017.

Liars, Leakers, and Liberals: Exposing the Plot to Destroy the Trump Campaign and Then the Trump Presidency, #1 *New York Times* Best Seller, Judge Jeanine Pirro, 2017.

The Diversity Delusion: How Race and Gender Pandering Corrupt the University and Undermine Our Culture, Heather MacDonald, a *New York Times* Best Selling Author, 2018.

Trump's America: The Truth About Our Nation's Great Comeback, #1 National Bestseller, Newt Gingrich, 2018.

Unfreedom of the Press: Fake News Reporting Today is Destroying Freedom of the Press from Within, Mark Levin, 2019

Radicals, Resistance and Revenge: The Left's Plot to Remake America, Judge Jeanine Pirro, a *New York Times* Best Selling Author, 2019

Power Grab: The Liberal Scheme to Undermine Trump, The GOP, and Our Republic, a *New York Times* Bestselling Author of The Deep State, Jason Chaffetz, 2019

The Case for Trump: Victor Davis Hanson, Stanford Professor and Classicist, Author of twenty-two books on war, ancient and modern … this man has perspective! 2019

Why Meadow Died: The People and Policies That Created the Parkland Shooter and Endanger America's Students, Andrew Pollack (Meadow's Father) and Max Eden, 2019. The politically correct "people" he is referring to are all liberal democrats.

Power Hungry: The Myths of Green Energy and the Real Fuels of the Future, Robert Bryce, Author of Gusher of Lies, 2010. The left has weaponized the weather with climate change alarmism, and they've done the same with energy production. The real purpose is furthering their revolution, not the climate or energy.

The Deliberate Corruption of Climate Science: Dr. Tim Ball exposes the malicious misuse of climate science as it was distorted by dishonest brokers to advance the political aspirations of the progressive left, Tim Ball, PhD, 2014.

Climate Change—The Facts: Edited by Alan Moran, a compilation of writings from dozens of esteemed climate scientists like Ian Plimer and Richard Lindzen, 2015

The Climate Report—The National Climate Assessment— Impacts, Risks, and Adaptation in the United States, U.S. Global Change and Research Program, 2018.

Climate Change Reconsidered II: Center for Study of Carbon Dioxide and Global Change and Science and Environment Policy Project, published by The Heartland Institute, 2019 A seven-hundred-and-sixty-five-page product of the Non-Governmental International Panel on Climate Change (NIPCC), created in 2003 by Dr. S. Fred Singer to provide an independent review of the reports of the United Nations IPCC. Over a hundred scientists, scholars, and experts concluded, "The global war on energy freedom, which commenced in earnest in the 1980s and reached a fever pitch in the second decade of the twenty-first century, was never founded on sound science or economics. The world's policy makers ought to acknowledge that truth and end that war."

And a website the reader interested in Climate Change should visit is: **www.petitionproject.org**.